Dr. Kennedy shows through the life and times of Gideon how ordinary people can accomplish extraordinary things when they follow His lead and not depend on our own strength and skills. This is an area where too many Christians remain stuck. As Dr. Kennedy states: "Gideon had knowledge of God, but he did not connect his knowledge to God's faithfulness." Throughout his book, Dr. Kennedy uses scriptural references to show how the disconnection between God and His people continually leads them to a "dead end." In this book, the reader will clearly see, as if they are looking in a mirror, what happens when God's people abandon their faith in Him and are motivated to action by their fear of what they don't understand or cannot see.

I especially like the sample prayers the author gives at the end of most chapters. These prayers give me a place to start and stop whenever I pray in general or about something in particular. The prayer examples (praying aids) help me focus my attention on the purpose of my prayer and on what I really want to say without being redundant or without feeling as if I have left something out.

Timeless Insights from the Book of Judges should be required reading for all true believers and for those who sometimes wonder *"where God is and does He really know what I am going through?"* This book is a handy antidote for life's "traps" that cause us to trust the "Bird in the Hand" rather than "the one that is in the bush." Too many times we discover this proverbial "bird in our hand" is dead, has no practical use or is an illegal catch. Dr. Kennedy's book helps us understand how God interacts with His creation, what He expects from His people and how He uses examples, situations and conditions to enrich the quality of our lives as He draws us closer Himself. I strongly recommend this book to all who want to grow in their faith in the Lord.

Dr. Robert Lewis, Jr.
Professor, University of La Verne
Elder, Mt. Zion Church of Ontario, Calif.

Timeless
Insights
from the
Book of Judges

How to Function in God's Eternal Plan
in a Compromising Culture

BRIAN E. KENNEDY

WESTBOW
PRESS®
A DIVISION OF THOMAS NELSON
& ZONDERVAN

Scripture taken from the NEW AMERICAN STANDARD BIBLE®, Copyright © 1960, 1962, 1963, 1968, 1971, 1972, 1973, 1975, 1977, 1995 by The Lockman Foundation. Used by permission.

Scriptures marked KJV are taken from the KING JAMES VERSION (KJV): KING JAMES VERSION, public domain.

WestBow Press books may be ordered through booksellers or by contacting:

WestBow Press
A Division of Thomas Nelson & Zondervan
1663 Liberty Drive
Bloomington, IN 47403
www.westbowpress.com
1 (866) 928-1240

Because of the dynamic nature of the Internet, any web addresses or links contained in this book may have changed since publication and may no longer be valid. The views expressed in this work are solely those of the author and do not necessarily reflect the views of the publisher, and the publisher hereby disclaims any responsibility for them.

Any people depicted in stock imagery provided by Thinkstock are models, and such images are being used for illustrative purposes only. Certain stock imagery © Thinkstock.

ISBN: 978-1-5127-7084-1 (sc)
ISBN: 978-1-5127-7085-8 (hc)
ISBN: 978-1-5127-7083-4 (e)

Library of Congress Control Number: 2016921630

Print information available on the last page.

WestBow Press rev. date: 2/7/2017

Dedicated to my parents

Contents

Foreword

Times have changed.

And I'm not just talking about the new marriage culture, codified by the Supreme Court's decision in Obergefell v. Hodges or the fact that current culture no longer views gender as binary. Times have changed—it seems as if there is no longer a moral north star guiding our culture—people are no longer doing what is "right," they are doing what seems right in their own eyes.

Actually, times have not changed, have they? During the days of the Judges, people were doing exactly the same thing; they were doing what seemed right in their own eyes. It was the Wild, Wild West of biblical times.

In *Timeless Insights from the Book of Judges,* Dr. Brian Kennedy points to the guiding North Star. He reminds his readers that God was firmly on His throne in the days of the Judges—and in ours. He calls on God's people to live the gospel's transformative power (1 Cor 6:11) and proclaim it boldly (Rom 1:16) in our world.

Instead of pining for the days when Christianity was the cultural norm, we will live the light (Matt. 5:14) in the darkness, among those who are doing what seems right in their own eyes.

Remember, the light shines brightest on the darkest night.

Jim Wilson,
Gateway Seminary
Professor of Leadership Development
Director of the Doctor of Ministry Program

Acknowledgments

I am forever indebted to my father, Bradford Kennedy (already in heaven), for pulling me aside when I was young and scolding me for not giving my best to my education. Daddy explained that he wished he could have gone to school and learned how to read, but his father took him out of school in the third grade to work on the farm. Daddy, close to tears, got inside my heart as he explained that he worked two jobs, sacrificed for all eight of his children, and taught us to work so that we could have the education he could not have.

Mom, you were our domestic engineer and creatively guided our spiritual and secular foundation so that we could succeed in the university, in the church, and in society. God used my daddy and mother to motivate me to enjoy learning.

To the love of my life, Hilda, and the four "little people"—Brian Jr., Evelyn, Lelia, and Joshua—I love each of you deeply, and I thank you for your prayers and endless support. Hilda, your deep desire for me to write and your loving encouragement drives me to excel more than you will ever imagine. Your graciousness, thoughtfulness, and smile continue to pierce my heart. With your support and sacrifices throughout our marriage, God has allowed us to see another milestone. God obviously knew what he was doing when he brought you into my life. My love for you continues to grow deeper.

To my church family, Mount Zion Church, in Ontario, California, my time as your pastor started in 1998 but seems like a lifetime. You are more than a congregation to me; you are my beloved family. I took note of your loving support of me from the very beginning. Thank you for your ongoing support. I look forward to the way in which our Lord will use this book to expand our participation in kingdom building. My mother rejoices over your love for Hilda, the children, and me. You are a pastor's dream church. Thank you.

To my San Diego parent's Ilan and Ruby Gordon; my Los Angeles mother, Margret Davis; and my families at Saint Paul Baptist Church, Sacramento; Calvary Baptist Church, San Diego; South Los Angeles Baptist Church (now merged with Christ Second Baptist Church) in Long Beach; and Evening Star Baptist Church in Los Angeles, where would I be without you. You continue to love me as your own son, and I will never forget you.

Dr. Ephraim Williams, Dr. S. M. Lockridge (in heaven), Dr. William Brent (in heaven), and Pastor Curtis Morris, I thank God for your pouring into my life. God put some of you inside of me, and He uses what I learned from you in my practice of ministry.

To Charles W. Colson (now in heaven), Tom Pratt, Alan K. Chambers, Harold Brinkley, Dr. Donald Cheek, Dr. Jeffrey Johnson, John Perkins, Daniel Van Ness, and the entire prison fellowship family, thanks for being an unforgettable family (the 1980s and '90s were a time of great growth for me). "Chuck" never flinched in his confidence in hiring me and reassuring me as I represented the ministry in Los Angeles. During my time with Prison Fellowship, God taught me to stay humble and trust Him in unusual circumstances. I would have crashed and burned in the pastorate without that experience.

I thank Dr. Jim Wilson for recruiting me to Gateway Seminary for the doctor of ministry (DMin) program. I thank the Golden Gate professors and my cohort members for intellectual and spiritual advancement, camaraderie, and spirited and thoughtful discussion during each seminar.

I also thank Pastor Glenn Jones, who introduced me to Dr. George Moore, Dr. James Rosscup, and the Talbot School of Theology family. The Talbot professors, led by Dr. George C. Moore as my mentor, laid a theological foundation that prepared me to thrive academically and serve in ministry anywhere in the world. Dr. James Rosscup, Dr. Robert Saucy, Dr. Jim Conway, Dr. Neil Anderson, and Dr. Henry Holloman helped me grow up in graduate school very quickly.

A special thanks to the late Pastor Floyd Johnson, Dr. Robert L. Lewis Jr., Dr. George C. Moore, and my heart, Hilda J. Kennedy, for constantly encouraging me to get started on writing and following through with professional help.

To God be the glory for the things He has done, is doing, and will do through this book.

Thank you President Jeff Iorg for inviting me to join the Gateway Seminary faculty as a Preaching Professor. Teaching at the graduate level is a dream come true.

Introduction

Does the Bible have timeless insights into a compromising culture? The obvious answer is yes. Amazingly, there are close similarities between the compromises we see in our current culture and those mentioned in the Bible. In the book of Judges, God is very honest regarding the spiritual decline of Israel after the death of Joshua. In Judges, we see many recurring themes that highlight the poor spiritual condition of Israel. The tribes of Judah, Benjamin, Joseph, Manasseh, Ephraim, Zebulun, Asher, Naphtali, and Dan did not drive out the inhabitants in their assigned territories.

By living with the inhabitants in the land, the children of Israel started to compromise and blend into the culture and practiced idol worship and immorality in the Promised Land. Four times in the book of Judges, we hear these words: "In those days there was no king in Israel" (Judges 17:6; 18:1; 19:1; 21:25). In addition, twice we see these words: "In those days there was no king in Israel; every man did what was right in his own eyes" (Judges 17:6; 21:25).

As the generation after Joshua practiced all kinds of spiritual wickedness, we see another recurring theme (six times): "The sons of Israel did what was evil in the sight of the Lord." Then on the seventh time, God said, "As soon as Gideon died, Israel played the harlot" (Judges 8:33).

What was the cause of Israel's unfaithfulness to God? Did God abandon them? Did Israel suffer from a famine or drought after they arrived in the Promised Land and so they got discouraged?

Did God somehow not keep His promise to them? God was not the problem. Here are the reasons listed in Judges regarding Israel's unfaithfulness to God:

- They forgot the Lord their God and served idol gods (3:7b).
- They did evil in the sight of the Lord (3:12b).
- They disobeyed God regarding the idols of the land (6:7–10).
- They did not remember the Lord who delivered them (8:34–35).
- They forgot about God and served idols (10:6b).

Disrespecting God by forgetting about him and worshiping idol gods was Israel's main problem.

What did God do when Israel did evil in His sight? Look at another recurring theme.

- God sold them into the hands of the Mesopotamians for eight years (Judges 3:8b).
- God used the Moabites to oppress them for eighteen years (Judges 3:12–13).
- God used the Canaanites to oppress them for twenty years (Judges 4:2–3).
- God used the Midianites to bring Israel low for seven years (Judges 6:1b, 3–6).
- God used the Philistines and Ammonites to afflict and crush them for eighteen years (Judges 10:8).
- God used the Philistines to oppress them for forty years (Judges 13:1).

You would think that after 111 years of six different punishments, somebody in the nation of Israel would have concluded that enough was enough and they needed to change.

Did Israel respond to God when He punished them? Look at another recurring theme in the book of Judges.

- The sons of Israel cried to the Lord (3:9a).
- The sons of Israel cried to the Lord (3:15).
- The sons of Israel cried to the Lord (4:3).
- The sons of Israel cried to the Lord (6:7).
- The sons of Israel cried out to the Lord, confessing their sin (10:10).
- The sons of Israel put away their idol gods and served the Lord (10:16a).
- The sons of Israel recognized Philistine rule over them (15:11).

Did God not hear Israel's cry and respond? Yes, he did. Look at another recurring theme.

- The Lord raised up a deliverer named Othniel for forty years (Judges 3:9b).
- The Lord raised up a deliverer named Ehud (Judges 3:15b).
- The Lord raised up Shamgar, who destroyed six hundred Philistines (Judges 3:31).
- The Lord raised up a deliverer named Deborah, the prophetess (Judges 4:4).
- The Lord raised up a deliverer named Gideon (Judges 6:11–40).
- The Lord raised up Tola, who judged for twenty-three years (Judges 10:2).
- The Lord raised up Jair, who judged for twenty-two years (Judges 10:3).

- The Lord said, "Let the gods you have chosen deliver you" (Judges 10:13–14). God said this when Israel got on His "last nerve" with their roller-coaster religion.
- The Lord could no longer bear to see the misery of Israel and raised up a deliverer named Jephthah, who judged seven years (Judges 10:16).
- The Lord raised up Ibzan who judged seven years (Judges 12:9).
- The Lord raised up Elon, who judged ten years (Judges 12:11).
- The Lord raised up Abdon, who judged eight years (Judges 12:14).
- The Lord raised up Samson, who judged twenty years (Judges 15:20).

In all the drama presented in the book of Judges, we see God doing His eternal work in a compromising culture. Despite their behavior, God does not give up on His children. God spanked some but raised up others to deliver those who cried out to Him, all while working His eternal plan to reconcile the world to Him.

In the book of Judges, we see God doing His eternal work with a variety of people. Let us watch God as He prepared Gideon to participate in His eternal work in a compromising culture.

CHAPTER 1

God Took Time to Clarify
Gideon's Hopeless Thinking

Judges 6:11–16

The first thing God did in preparing Gideon to participate in His eternal work was to clarify Gideon's hopeless thinking.

When God called Gideon, He targeted Gideon's area of doubt.

> Then the angel of the Lord came and sat under the oak that was in Ophrah, which belonged to Joash the Abiezrite as his son Gideon was beating out wheat in the wine press in order to save it from the Midianites. The angel of the Lord appeared to him and said to him, "The Lord is with you, O valiant warrior." Then Gideon said to him, "O my lord, if the Lord is with us, why then has all this happened to us? And where are all His miracles which our fathers told us about, saying, 'Did not the Lord bring us up from Egypt?' But now the Lord has abandoned us and given us into the hand of Midian." (Judges 6:11–13)

God appeared when Gideon thought God had abandoned Israel. Look at the verse 12 again: "The Lord is with you, O valiant warrior."

Being in a state of oppression, Gideon and the children of Israel were weak and helpless against the Midianites. Then God showed up and called Gideon strong. "Hey, strong warrior!"

In verse 13, Gideon questioned God's power for miracles. Essentially, Gideon's response to God was, "If God is with us, where are all the miracles that He worked for our fathers? Egypt was a strong country, and God delivered us from them. Why is God not working an Egypt-sized miracle to deliver us from the Midianites?" Gideon saw hopelessness in Israel's oppression.

Gideon saw only hopelessness. He felt that since the Lord was not working any miracles to deliver him and Israel, He had abandoned them—and that was why Midian had made them weak and helpless.

What was Gideon doing when the angel of the Lord spoke to him? Every time the children of Israel's crops were ready to harvest, the Midianites came in and destroyed them, and they killed the sheep, oxen, and donkeys. The Midianites cut off Israel's food supply.

Therefore, Gideon was secretly harvesting wheat and storing it in the wine press, hiding it from the Midianites. Gideon's hiding food describes the hopelessness in Israel at the time.

Someone told Gideon about Israel's history, so you might imagine what was on Gideon's mind. He must have thought, *I heard that God could work miracles and stop all this oppression, but He has not done it. Therefore, God must not love us anymore. Surely God has abandoned us. God left us out here alone.*

What was Gideon missing? Gideon had knowledge of God, but he did not connect his knowledge to God's faithfulness. In the history of Israel, God always was faithful to Israel, even when Israel was unfaithful. God could have destroyed Israel several times for disrespecting Him, but God remembered His promise to Abraham—to bless the nations through his seed.

God had to help Gideon make a connection in his thinking. In order to help Gideon with his doubt and discouragement, God met Gideon in person. Gideon called God to do what he thought God was *not* going to do.

"The LORD looked at him and said, 'Go in this your strength and deliver Israel from the hand of Midian. Have I not sent you?'" (Judges 6:14).

In other words, Gideon—Mr. Hopeless, Mr. Negative—claimed that God had abandoned him. But God replied that He had chosen Gideon to bring hope back to the nation of Israel—and to prove that God had not abandoned them.

Let's consider that again: "'Go in this your strength!' commanded the Lord. 'Deliver Israel from the hand of Midian! Have I not sent you?'"

Notice how God can call us when we are deep in doubt to do the very thing we have convinced ourselves that God will not do. God also introduced His miracle-working power. "Go in your strength. (I will give it to you.) Deliver Israel from Midian. (I will be with you.) I sent, and I when I send, I will supply." God will meet us right where we are to clarify our hopeless thinking.

Look at Gideon's response to God's call: "He said to Him, 'O Lord, how shall I deliver Israel? Behold, my family is the least in Manasseh, and I am the youngest in my father's house'" (Judges 6:15). Gideon must have thought, *God, I am just not the one. God, why in the world would you pick me, the least likely person to deliver anybody or anything, let alone a nation?*

This response is common for us today. Instead of focusing on the miracle-working power of God in our lives, we focus on our own abilities and on what we cannot do in our human strength.

God's call is not about our family history, our birthdays (God knows our ages), or what we think we can or cannot do. God's call is not about comparing ourselves with others.

God's call is about God's including us in His eternal work in a compromising culture. God chooses to use us to bring hope to the hopeless and to draw people to Him.

When God calls, you cannot focus on "me, myself, and I"—you must focus on the call. You must focus on what part God wants you to play in His huge eternal plan. God called you because your part is important to Him. Others may not notice, but God sees your part as valuable—and He included you.

"But the LORD said to him, 'Surely I will be with you, and you shall defeat Midian as one man'" (Judges 6:16).

What does the Bible say that God can do with the least likely person? God can take His presence and power and transform the least likely into the most likely person. He can transform the weak into the strong, the loser into the winner, and the hopeless into the hopeful.

How does God do this transforming work? With His presence and power.

"Surely I will be with you" (Judges 6:16). That is God's presence.

"You shall defeat Midian as one man" (Judges 6:16). That is God's power.

God is saying, *I will make the impossible very simple. You will defeat the powerful nation of Midian as if you were fighting only one person.*

I recommend that you try to let go of your situation! Stop trying to fix things that are out of your control. You tried for years, and the situation is still broken.

Step back, and ask God to stand in you and work through you. Ask God to fill you afresh with His Holy Spirit so that you have His power activated in your life.

Let God's presence and power transform you from weakness to strength, from shyness to boldness, from helplessness to courage, from giving up to finishing.

Let God transform you, in the midst of your impossible circumstances, from a doubter to a believer, from a detriment to an asset, and from a complainer to an encourager. Let Him transform you from depressed to excited, from traumatized to stable, from tormented to peaceful, from lazy to energetic, from passive to active, from enslaved to free, and from down-and-out to up and about.

Gideon suffered with the same problem that many of us have today. In our compromising culture, we feel helpless and as if God has left us here to fend for ourselves. God allowed the Supreme Court to legalize same-sex marriage. God allowed a bisexual to pastor a church. God allowed the Supreme Court to take prayer out of schools. God allowed the United States court system to sentence an innocent person to life in prison. God allowed this Christian-based nation to legalize slavery. God allowed so-called Christians to terrorize American citizens through hate groups such as the Ku Klux Klan. God allowed the 9/11 terrorist attack on America. God allowed the Boston Marathon bombing. God allowed the murder of nine Christians in Charleston, South Carolina. God allowed this tragedy and that tragedy. Has God abandoned us?

Even when things have gone from bad to worse, and some of God's children have compromised and blended into the culture, God has not abandoned His children. God does not ignore our circumstances. God hears our cries and will respond to us as He works His eternal plan.

In the midst of a compromising culture, God wants to transform us into His mighty warriors to take His message and deliver people from oppression and their lost conditions.

Stop being stuck on you and your plan. Focus on God's calling, which includes you in His eternal plan to reconcile the world to Himself. God is working on eternal solutions in a messed-up world.

Just as God took time to clarify Gideon's hopeless thinking, He will take time to clarify your hopeless thinking.

Let God get you beyond your hopeless thinking and clearly show you where you fit into His eternal plan. Work on God's team as God works in this compromising culture.

CHAPTER 2

God Allowed Gideon to Test
Him for Reassurance

Judges 6:17–24

How does God do eternal work in a compromised culture? A compromising culture is a society in which people claim to know God, but they choose to reject God's Word in their policies, values, decision-making, and way of life. They are the Sunday churchgoers who sing and pray and then go home to cuss and fight, abuse drugs and alcohol, make unjust judgments, negotiate unfairly, gamble away the family money, lie and steal, take more than they should, engage in sexual immorality, and live as if they did not hear anything in church—and they dare anyone to challenge them. We live in a compromising culture.

When evil seems to prevail and laws go against what God says in His Word, and when it seems like good is faced with one defeat after another, how in the world does God do an eternal work in a compromised culture? How can we be sure that God is at work? How can we be sure that God will use us to make a difference?

If you are not sure, God will help you with reassurance. Gideon was quick to seek God for reassurance. Look at how God allowed Gideon to test Him.

"So Gideon said to Him, 'If now I have found favor in Your sight, then show me a sign that it is You who speak with me'" (Judges 6:17).

God was right there in Gideon's presence, speaking and clearing up his hopeless thinking. In addition, Gideon said, Lord, I want to be sure that you are the One speaking to me. Show me something to prove that I have found favor in your sight and that you want to use me as you said. I just need to be sure that I am not tricking myself into answering a call that you did not make.

Don't get mad at Gideon for asking for a sign. If America was oppressed for seven years by a nation that it was meant to conquer, and God called you to help, you too would want reassurance.

Whatever we think about Gideon's asking for a sign is irrelevant. What is relevant is what God did with Gideon's request. Did God become angry and kill Gideon? Did God simply walk away and choose someone else? What do you want God to do with you when you're trying to get some reassurance?

God engaged Gideon because of his sincere heart. "'Please do not depart from here, until I come back to You, and bring out my offering and lay it before You.'" And He said, 'I will remain until you return'" (Judges 6:18).

Gideon must have thought, *God, I know you will accept a certain kind of worship. I know that if I bring the right offering to you and lay it before You, You will accept it, and you will reveal yourself.*

Idol gods cannot respond to anything a person brings to them. Idol gods receive ongoing maintenance by the humans who worship them. Gideon knew the true God would respond to his offering. He had to be sure he was dealing with the true and living God, and he said, "Hold up! Whoever you are, I will be right back."

God is always looking at our hearts, and Gideon's willingness to bring an appropriate offering to seek God's reassurance was an indication of his sincerity.

"Then Gideon went in and prepared a young goat and unleavened bread from an ephah of flour; he put the meat in a basket and the broth in a pot, and brought them out to him under the oak and presented them" (Judges 6:19).

How did the true God respond?

"The angel of God said to him, 'Take the meat and the unleavened bread and lay them on this rock, and pour out the broth.' And he did so. Then the angel of the LORD put out the end of the staff that was in his hand and touched the meat and the unleavened bread; and fire sprang up from the rock and consumed the meat and the unleavened bread. Then the angel of the LORD vanished from his sight" (Judges 6:20–21).

God had Gideon act in faith and rearrange the way he brought his offering to God—move the bread and the meat, and pour out the broth. Gideon did not question God but acted in faith.

God responds to our acts of faith. The angel of the Lord caused fire to spring up from the rock and consumed the meat and the bread. This was God's way of accepting Gideon's offering and reassuring Gideon that he was engaging the true and living God.

When God sees you giving your offering in faith, He will respond to reassure you.

God's peace will reassure a fearful heart. "When Gideon saw that he was the angel of the LORD, he said, 'Alas, O Lord GOD! For now I have seen the angel of the LORD face to face.' The LORD said to him, 'Peace to you, do not fear; you shall not die'" (Judges 6:22–23).

Gideon was afraid because he engaged God face-to-face; he thought he would die because no one can see God's face and live (Exodus 33:20).

With whom was Gideon dealing in the person of the angel of the Lord? Because God is Spirit, and humans cannot see God face-to-face and live, and because ordinary angels do not accept worship, and this angel of the Lord did accept worship from Gideon, who was He?

The angel of the Lord was none other than the pre-incarnate Christ. Jesus, who is equal to God, came in human form and engaged humankind before he came to the earth as Mary's baby. Jesus was in the fiery furnace with the three Hebrew boys (Daniel 3:24–25).

Jesus showed up and reassured Joshua, as the captain of God's army (Joshua 5:13–15).

Jesus showed up and wrestled with Jacob and then changed his name to Israel (Genesis 32:24–30).

Jesus also showed up in your situation and made you a child of God so that you now have abundant life (Ephesians 2:1–10; John 10:10).

Do you need a sign? Call Jesus, and watch Him show up in your life.

When Gideon realized that the angel of the Lord was God, he was afraid, but God again spoke to Gideon and reassured him with peace. God's peace will reassure a fearful heart. Remember what God said to Gideon, "Peace to you!" "Do not be afraid!" "You will not die!"

What part of your circumstances brings fear to your heart? God has peace for you. In fact, God said He gives perfect peace when your mind locks in on Him because of your trust in Him (Isaiah 26:3).

Trust is necessary to have God's peace, and God's peace is necessary to conquer a fearful heart.

What happens when God calms our hearts with His peace? "Then Gideon built an altar there to the LORD and named it The LORD is Peace. To this day it is still in Ophrah of the Abiezrites" (Judges 6:24).

Worship naturally flows when God's peace fills our hearts.

Stop and worship God for the miracles He works in your life.

God allowed Gideon to put Him to the test for the purpose of reassurance. God indulged Gideon because God saw his sincere heart.

Before you say that you know God sent you to do this or that, be sure to check that God is the one speaking.

Before you quit because you're afraid of what is in front of you, stop and make sure God is in the situation. Put your total trust in God, and let God remove your fear with His peace.

Before you move forward with reassurance, stop and worship God for His call on your life. Stop and worship God's transforming you into a strong warrior for Him. Stop and worship God for taking away your fear and giving you His peace and for including you in His eternal plan.

When forming new relationships, what two discussion topics are we advised to avoid? Religion and politics. That's because our views about religion and politics go deeper than superficial questions, such as "Where were you born?" and "What are your dreams?" Our views about religion and politics reveal our personal values—how we actually feel about people and things and how we live.

We avoid values-driven topics so we don't offend anyone—a romantic partner, for example, or someone we hope will give us a large contract or a new job. We want to stay on people's good side.

The challenge we have as Christians is that God chose us to participate in His eternal work in a compromising culture. What we say from God's Word is not always popular. People who do not share our values may misunderstand, criticize, contradict, and persecute us; they prefer to cut us out of the action. Despite how people say they love us and our work, people who support a compromising culture never fully accept Christians.

God is very kind to include us in His eternal work in a culture that seems out of control. Tragedy, injustice, idol worship, immorality, pestilence, drought, war, terrorism, domestic violence, sickness, death, poverty, greed, and crime seem to be unmanageable, but God still has an eternal plan to reconcile the world to Him, and He chooses to use us in His plan.

God chose people to deal with the impossible and to do what people thought God was not going to do. God dealt with Gideon and got Gideon ready to bring hope to a hopeless situation. Since God chooses us to participate with Him in a compromising culture, we need to know how God does His work.

CHAPTER 3

God Tested Gideon for Loyalty

Judges 6:25–32

Before God used Gideon to deliver Israel, He tested Gideon for loyalty. Loyalty is faithfulness or devotion to someone. Israel had a loyalty problem.

Look at the spiritual condition of Israel, as described in the book of Judges.

- Israel forgot the Lord their God and served idol gods (3:7b).
- Israel did evil in the sight of the Lord (3:12b).
- Israel disobeyed God regarding the idols of the land (6:7–10).
- Israel did not remember the Lord who delivered them (8:34–35).
- Israel forgot about God and served idols (10:6b).

Look in the book of Judges at what God did to Israel for disrespecting Him and worshiping idol gods.

- God sold Israel into the hands of the Mesopotamians for eight years (3:8b).
- God used the Moabites to oppress Israel for eighteen years (3:12–13).

- God used the Canaanites to oppress Israel for twenty years (4:2–3).
- God used the Midianites to bring Israel low for seven years (6:1b, 3–6).
- God used the Philistines and Ammonites to afflict and crush Israel eighteen years (10:8).
- God used the Philistines to oppress Israel for forty years (13:1).

God gave Israel 111 years of six different punishments because of their disrespectful behavior of chasing after idol gods. Israel had a loyalty problem before God.

"Now on the same night the LORD said to him, 'Take your father's bull and a second bull seven years old, and pull down the altar of Baal which belongs to your father, and cut down the Asherah that is beside it; and build an altar to the LORD your God on the top of this stronghold in an orderly manner, and take a second bull and offer a burnt offering with the wood of the Asherah which you shall cut down'" (Judges 6:25–26).

God's command here tested Gideon's obedience to God over family. Before God put Gideon out there, God wanted Gideon to have made up his mind, such that he would obey Him, despite what his family said or did.

You've heard the phrase, blood is thicker than water. Well, our relationship with God and our obedience to Him is supposed to be thicker than blood.

Will you obey God, despite compromising family members? Whatever your family has planned, if the family plan compromises your Christian values, are you willing to obey God over your family?

How far are you willing to go with this Christian thing? God delivered you from drug addiction and alcohol abuse. God delivered you from fighting and cussing, and mistreating people, and unfair business practices, and other ungodly practices.

Now that your family wants you to participate in some things that God says are clearly wrong, what will you do? Will you obey God or obey your family?

Are you willing to share your Christian testimony and lovingly be with your family without participating in their sin? Are you willing to eat with them and be a light among them as they promote darkness?

You might be the only witness for Christ your family trusts. Will you be God's representative, as God desires to use you in His eternal plan to save your family?

Will you pass God's loyalty test?

Compromising and being popular is much easier than obeying some of God's commands, as His commands often will counter the compromising culture. God's Word does not go along with people who want to leave God out, ignore His Word, and do their own thing.

"Then Gideon took ten men of his servants and did as the LORD had spoken to him; and because he was too afraid of his father's household and the men of the city to do it by day, he did it by night" (Judges 6:27).

I love the Word of God because God did not fill the Bible with plastic saints. Bible characters are real people with real issues. Family life in Israel during Bible times was like real life today. Gideon showed respect for his father and family. We see in Judges 6:11 that Gideon cared for his family and worked to provide food for them because the Midianites regularly destroyed Israel's food supply.

Gideon's father, his father's household, and the men of the city were all faithful worshipers of the idol gods on Gideon's daddy's property, and Gideon knew about this ungodly practice.

Think about this: Gideon's daddy was the man—he was a source of food, had a large household, and had the idol gods Baal and the Asherah on his property. Gideon's daddy was friends with the men of the city. People came to Gideon's daddy's house to worship idol gods. Gideon had a good reason to be afraid to touch his daddy's altar with those idol gods, let alone tear them down and build something different. The true God, who clearly revealed Himself to Gideon, commanded Gideon to destroy His daddy's altar, where his idol gods Baal and the Asherah were on display.

James Newell, in the *Holman Bible Dictionary*, noted that Baal was lord of the Canaanite religion, and Baal worshipers supposedly could see Baal in thunderstorms. People worshiped Baal as the god who provided fertility (rain for the crops).[1]

The Asherah was a fertility goddess and supposedly the mother of Baal, whose worship was concentrated in Syria and Canaan. (The Asherah was a wooden object that represented her.)[2]

It was as if God said, "Gideon, your daddy is a ringleader for Israel's idol worship, and before I can use you, I need you to make a clean break from the idol worship happening in your daddy's household. Destroy your father's altar and those idols, build another altar, and make a sacrifice that is pleasing to me!"

Gideon was afraid of his daddy, but he respected God more, so he obeyed God, despite his fear.

Gideon destroyed his father's altar at night, and sure enough, just as Gideon expected, the men of the city were upset.

> When the men of the city arose early in the morning,
> behold, the altar of Baal was torn down, and the

---

[1] James Newell, "Baal," ed. Chad Brand et al., *Holman Illustrated Bible Dictionary* (Nashville, TN: Holman Bible Publishers, 2003), 152.
[2] James Newell, *Holman Illustrated Bible Dictionary*, 125.

Asherah, which was beside it, was cut down, and the second bull was offered on the altar which had been built. They said to one another, "Who did this thing?" And when they searched about and inquired, they said, "Gideon the son of Joash did this thing." Then the men of the city said to Joash, "Bring out your son, that he may die, for he has torn down the altar of Baal, and indeed, he has cut down the Asherah which was beside it." (Judges 6:28–30)

Do not mess with compromising people's idol gods! Do not mess with God's people when they are in sin and in trouble with God—they will bite your head off. Compromising people will persecute challengers. When people know they are wrong, they do not want any reminders.

Instead of getting up early to worship the true and living God, the men of the city of Ophrah got up, looking for Baal and the Asherah. Instead of looking higher to see that an altar and sacrifice was made for the God of Israel, these men looked low to see their handmade, false gods, and they became angry enough to kill Gideon for bringing their attention to the true and living God. They confronted Joash, Gideon's father, "bring out your son that he may die, for he has torn down the altar of Baal."

According to Judges 6:7, the sons of Israel had just cried out to God because God was punishing them for worshipping idol gods. Judges 6:30 reveals, however, that not everyone cried out to God for help. Despite God's spanking the nation of Israel, some people were still content with disobeying God and worshipping their idol gods.

Not everyone wants God to deliver him or her from sin.

As family members, friends, coworkers, fellow students, and even this country go deeper into idol worship and immorality, and you declare what God says, be ready for persecution.

People—especially religious, churchgoing people who know right from wrong but who compromise and are caught up in sin—know they are in sin. Guilt and shame is all over their countenances. Yet if you challenge them in their wrongdoings, they will persecute you. They will fight God and fight you for challenging their ungodly practices.

For His redemptive purposes, God overrides human plans. What happened when the men of the city sought to kill God's man Gideon? God stepped in and overrode their plans. God loves humans so much that He will not allow humans to interfere with His eternal plan to save humans. "But Joash said to all who stood against him, 'Will you contend for Baal, or will you deliver him? Whoever will plead for him shall be put to death by morning. If he is a god, let him contend for himself, because someone has torn down his altar'" (Judges 6:31).

What? An unexpected response for the owner of the idol gods? How did that happen?

God controls the hearts of humankind. "The king's heart is like channels of water in the hand of the LORD; He turns it wherever He wishes" (Proverbs 21:1).

Yes, Joash was "the man" in his community, but God is the all-powerful God of the universe. When it seems that humankind is about to mess up what God has planned for His children, God demonstrates that He is still in control and will deliver His children!

Joash, Gideon's daddy, was deep into the culture of idol worship and could have turned on his own son and had him killed. This was not a light threat to Gideon or his dad. If Dad did not handle the situation correctly, the men of the city would have turned on him.

Despite Joash's worship of idol gods, God, in His faithfulness, intervened and gave Joash words of wisdom. "But Joash said to all who stood against him, 'Will you contend for Baal, or will you deliver him? Whoever will plead for him shall be put to death by morning. If he is a god, let him contend for himself, because someone has torn down his altar'" (Judges 6:31).

What is this? You want to kill somebody over the destruction of a god? If Baal is really a god, let him plead his own case and deal with his destruction by a mere mortal. In fact, all who try to kill somebody because their idol god could not fight for himself should die themselves.

God's purpose was to test Gideon, not have him killed (Judges 6:25–26, 14, 16). God was not going to let Gideon die after He called Gideon to be the deliverer to get the Midianites off the back of Israel.

One of the great lessons, as God tests our loyalty, is that as we humbly trust God in the test, God will faithfully exalt us. "Therefore on that day he named him Jerubbaal, that is to say, 'Let Baal contend against him,' because he had torn down his altar" (Judges 6:32).

Instead of people in the compromising culture killing him that day, God honored Gideon with a new name to remind people of Gideon's boldness against Baal worship and countering the compromising culture. God exalted Gideon and put Gideon's accusers in check.

God will make our enemies behave when they threaten us for challenging their disobedience to Him.

Another great lesson is that although Gideon was afraid, he did not run away. Despite any fear that comes over us, we should not run away. God will give us the strength we need when we stand strong for God.

We also learn from Gideon how to lay low as God fights for us. Yes, boldly stand there on God's side as God's representative. Yet, stay humble and lay low, as God sometimes uses even the least likely person to stand up and fight for us.

Remember this: the people who persecute you are often the people that God called you to help. Gideon would eventually deliver the people who had tried to kill him.

Hence, do not be so quick to write off your persecutors and the people who fight against you. Stand for God. Pursue God's calling on your life. Focus on letting God know, through your unquestioning obedience, that He can depend on you when he calls you. Pass the loyalty test!

Here is a personal prayer to help:

Lord, compromise is all around me. People close to me compromise. I even struggle with compromise myself. Please forgive me for anything I have done to compromise your high standards. Father, I thank you for not abandoning your people in a compromising culture. Lord, deal with me and build my relationship with you, such that you can use me to take a strong stand for you. Take away my fear with your peace, and intervene in the midst of persecution. I place my life and my total trust in your capable hands. Use me as a vessel of honor, sanctified and qualified for your use. I love you deeply. In the name of Jesus, I pray. Amen.

CHAPTER 4

Fulfilling God's Call without "I-Got-This-itis"

Judges 6:33–40

How many times have you used the expression "I got this"? What were you really thinking? Were you just kidding around with the person you were addressing, or did you really feel deep inside that you could handle the situation without anyone's help, including God's help?

When we lean on our own understanding, and venture out to handle our affairs, we leave God out and suffer with an old human sickness that I call "I-Got-This-itis."

We suffer with I-Got-This-itis when we possess an overconfidence in self, such that it attacks our daily dependence on God and tries to fulfill God's call on our lives by leaning on our own understanding.

Let me tell you something: do not ride a camel if you suffer with I-Got-This-itis because you will fall. From my personal experience, I know that you cannot become overconfident when riding a camel. I strongly recommend that you avoid texting while riding a camel.

In church, we want to put our best feet forward by appearing okay. Some of us act as if we do not have any challenges, and we act spiritual ("I got this"), but this fake mentality is a gigantic problem in the church today—many of us are just faking it and shaking it. The best way to deal with our issues and grow spiritually is to honestly look at ourselves, based on God's Word.

Going to church is like going to the doctor for checkups and treatments. Sometimes we have a great week of good spiritual health. Other times we come to church with serious spiritual issues that need a life-changing spiritual treatment.

God gave us a one-of-a-kind book, the Bible, which is full of teachings, places, events, and real people with victories and defeats. It tells us of their dealings with God and God's dealings with them. God wants us to look at our book and apply the eternal life lessons to our lives.

Let's look in the Bible at Gideon's life to see how Gideon fulfilled God's calling on his life without I-Got-This-itis. As we do, pay attention to how God and Gideon relate to each other. Pay attention to what you see and what you do not see in the scriptures. Then honestly look at yourself; how does what God reveals in His Word make you better?

Let's first see what could have happened after Gideon's big win. After a big win, I-Got-This-itis can lead to overconfidence in self, and Gideon had several things going for him that could have led him to suffer with I-Got-This-itis.

In Judges 6, the children of Israel were in trouble with God again for doing evil in God's sight. Israel disrespected God by worshipping idol gods; therefore, God handed them over to Midian for seven years. Midian was very cruel and ran Israel from their homes, such that they hid in the mountains and caves.

Midian also destroyed the food supply. When the crops were ready to harvest, Midian destroyed the crops and killed their sheep, oxen, and donkeys, and Israel became very poor in their oppression.

Israel cried out, and God sent a prophet to rebuke them for their evil practices, and then God sent the angel of the Lord to call Gideon to be Israel's deliverer.

When God called Gideon, He reassured Gideon that He was with him.

"Then the Angel of the LORD appeared to Gideon and said: 'The LORD is with you, mighty warrior'" (Judges 6:12).

"The LORD turned to him and said, 'Go in the strength you have and deliver Israel from the power of Midian. Am I not sending you?'" (Judges 6:14).

"'But I will be with you,' the LORD said to him. 'You will strike Midian down as if it were one man'" (Judges 6:16).

Gideon asked God for a sign to reassure him of the call to deliver Israel from Midian. God did what Gideon asked by responding to Gideon with fire. Gideon knew God was with him.

Gideon had another thing going for him; he had success under his belt.

God then put Gideon's loyalty to the test. He commanded Gideon to destroy his father's idol god altar and to build a proper altar and offer a sacrifice to the true God. Gideon was afraid of his father's household and the men of the city, so he waited until night to obey God's command. Then he successfully tore down his daddy's altar to idol gods.

Gideon had another thing going for him; he survived a death threat by an angry crowd.

Just as Gideon expected, the men of the city were upset and wanted to kill him for destroying their idol god altar and their idols. The people in the city had gathered at the home of Gideon's father to worship their idol gods, and now their gods were gone.

God intervened on Gideon's behalf and used Joash, Gideon's father, to challenge the angry men of the city to let Baal defend himself. "But Joash said to all who stood against him, 'Would you plead Baal's case for him? Would you save him? Whoever pleads his case will be put to death by morning! If he is a god, let him plead his own case because someone tore down his altar'" (Judges 6:31).

Gideon's experience was a genuine "Wow!" moment. His relatives tried to kill him, but God delivered him. After such a great victory, Gideon could have developed a serious case of I-Got-This-itis, but he did not. God shows us this part of Gideon's life so that we view Gideon as just as human as we are, and we see how Gideon refused to adopt the common human reaction to success: "I got this."

Where are you today? Did you get something right last week? Did you close a big deal recently? Did you win an argument? Did you get a big win?

Your recent victory is what perfectly positions you to declare in your heart, "I got this,"

What is the problem with becoming overconfident after getting an A on a test or after getting a big win? You will have more tests and more challenges in life. Just as God got you through your yesterday, you will need Him today and tomorrow. Therefore, do not allow I-Got-This-itis to blind you to your daily need to depend on God.

What lesson do we learn from Gideon in Judges 6? We learn that for each God-given assignment, we are to let God's Spirit take control. "Then all the Midianites and the Amalekites and the people of the east came together, and crossing the Jordan they encamped in the Valley of Jezreel. But the spirit of the LORD took possession of Gideon; and he sounded the trumpet, and the Abiezrites were called out to follow him. He sent messengers throughout all Manasseh, and they too were called out to follow him. He also sent messengers to Asher, Zebulun, and Naphtali, and they went up to meet them" (Judges 6:33–35).

God called Gideon to deliver Israel from the Midianites. Who were the Midianites?

- The Midianites are descendants of Keturah, Abraham's fourth wife (Genesis 25:1).
- The Midianites received Moses when he escaped from Egypt (Exodus 2:15).
- Moses married a Midianite woman named Zipporah (Exodus 2:21).
- Jethro, the priest of Midian, helped to restructure Israel (Exodus 18:14–24).
- A Midianite woman led Israel astray into sexual immorality (Numbers 25:6–18).
- The Midianites along with Moabites saw Israel as a threat and hired Balak to curse Israel before they arrived in the Promised Land (Numbers 22:4–7).

Once Israel arrived in the Promised Land, the Midianites joined up with the Amalekites and other people from the east to attack Israel. The Midianites proved how much they despised the Israelites by the seven years of cruel treatment recorded in Judges 6. Israel cried out, and God called Gideon to deal with Midian, who was then a fierce enemy of Israel.

Why did they attack the Israelites in the Valley of Jezreel? The International Coastal Highway entered the Valley of Jezreel at Megiddo. This important city guarded the main pass leading to the valley and was the scene of many battles. The name *Armageddon* ("Mountain of Megiddo") used in Revelation 16:16 recalls the numerous conflicts fought over control of this strategic valley.[3]

---

[3] Thomas V. Brisco, *Holman Bible Atlas*, Holman Reference (Nashville, TN: Broadman & Holman Publishers, 1998), 16.

Whoever controlled the Valley of Jezreel controlled the strategic trade routes from the Mediterranean Sea, to Egypt, and to kings of the East.

The Valley of Jezreel was also very fertile with food and water.

Tearing down his dad's altar was a loyalty test, not Gideon's calling (Judges 6:25–26). When Gideon tore down his father's idol god altar and destroyed his father's idols, the community went ballistic. Gideon struck at the heart of Israel's problem, which was idol worship. Yes, Israel had a sin problem, but notice in Judges 6:8 that God sent a prophet to deal with Israel's spiritual problem, and in Judges 6:14, God called Gideon to deal with Israel's military problem.

Can you see the real issue at hand? The children of Israel were facing a war against people who were determined to destroy them at a strategic location. Gideon had to avoid being stuck on yesterday's victory on his daddy's property. Gideon needed to answer God's call to be a great military leader.

Can you see how I-Got-This-itis could have moved Gideon into the business of tearing down idol god altars? Gideon could have become overconfident, leaned on his own understanding, and missed his true calling.

God called Gideon to deliver Israel from the Midianites, not dwell on his past victory and start a tear-down-idol-god-altars business.

This is a lesson for us: some of us are preoccupied with the wrong assignment. We are stuck on doing one thing, which is often good, but God really called us to something else.

Some of us are stuck in our relationships on the wrong things. We are holding on to the speeding tickets our wife got ten years ago and cannot see her true value to the family. She paid her tickets ten years ago and went to driver's school to improve her skills, but

I-Got-This-itis has us stuck on how we told her to slow down and how we need to keep her in check. We are stuck on the wrong assignment. Our assignment is not ticket counting and monitoring our wife's driving; it's to love our wife the way Christ loved the church and to cherish our relationships with our wife.

I-Got-This-itis can be defeated, but we must be willing to get out of the way and let God's Spirit work.

"So the Spirit of the Lord came upon Gideon; and he blew a trumpet, and the Abiezrites were called together to follow him. He sent messengers throughout Manasseh, and they also were called together to follow him; and he sent messengers to Asher, Zebulun, and Naphtali, and they came up to meet them" (Judges 6:34–35).

Gideon blew the trumpet to call his relatives for war (Judges 6:34). The very family members who were about to kill Gideon came out to follow Gideon into battle.

Gideon was from the Abiezrites. The Abiezrites were from the tribe of Manasseh and were given the territory by Joshua (Joshua 17:2), which included the city of Ophrah, where Gideon tore down his father's altar to Baal, and the Asherah.[4]

Gideon sent messengers to gather other tribes of Israel to follow Gideon into battle (Judges 6:35). The Spirit of God confirmed God's leading Gideon as people gathered.

Do you remember what Gideon said when God first called him? "O Lord, how shall I deliver Israel? Behold, my family is the least in Manasseh, and I am the youngest in my father's house" (Judges 6:15).

Gideon told God, "I am not your man. My family has no real influence since we are the least in Manasseh, and I am the youngest in my father's house. Who will listen to me?"

---

[4] Allen C. Myers, *The Eerdmans Bible Dictionary* (Grand Rapids, MI: Eerdmans, 1987), 6.

Do you know what makes the difference when God gives us a new assignment? It's the Spirit of the living God. The Spirit of the Lord came upon Gideon, and then Gideon functioned as a deliverer for the nation.

The Spirit of the living God took Gideon beyond his first major accomplishment on his daddy's property to leading the nation as their military leader. This was Gideon's true calling.

Yes, Gideon was right about his lack of influence. He was not capable of delivering Israel in his own strength. What made the difference? Gideon was willing and available for God to use him. Yes, Gideon started out slow, and yes, Gideon asked God for a sign so that he could be certain, but God saw Gideon's heart and his willingness to serve. Even after a major victory at his dad's house, Gideon clearly resisted the I-got-this mentality, and because he did, the Spirit of God came upon him and led him to fulfill God's call on his life.

The Spirit of God also will lead you to do thing related to your calling. What is the key to getting supernatural help in fulfilling your calling? You must resist the spirit of "I got this," and allow the Spirit of the living God to fall fresh on you and guide you.

Stay weak before God, like Gideon. Learn to resist knowing everything. Learn to recognize how limited you really are. Learn to open yourself up for God to guide you each step of the way. Stay open to each new assignment from God so that you can fulfill God's call on your life.

Has I-Got-This-itis led you into activities that are watering down your effectiveness? Did the Spirit of God lead you to overload your plate? You barely have time to take a shower and get out the door to the next thing and then the next thing. You come home dog-tired every day. You cannot spend quality time with your family because the next thing has your mind preoccupied.

Is the Spirit of God leading you to continue your bad habits? "Don't worry about my bad habits," you might say. "I got this." This is exactly the point of this chapter.

You will never fulfill your God-given purpose, never reach your full potential, never get to the right next assignment, and never accomplish the things that fulfill you as long as you continue to say, "I got this."

So what should you do? Repent! Yes, repent! Ask God to forgive you for being overconfident in yourself. Ask God to forgive you for leaving Him out and leaning on your own understanding.

Surprisingly, what I am doing is working out. I am getting around to things. I am getting things done. I believe that God is using what I am doing.

Yes, God is using what you are doing, but God did not call you to a barely-get-things-done life. God did not call you to coming in dog-tired every day. God did not call you to a body breakdown because of stress. God did not call you to taking pills for panic attacks from self-imposed stress. God did not call you to look tore up from the floor up because of stress.

We are not fooling God with all of our busy work! God did not put us under constant stress with all the stuff we're trying to do. We are suffering from a bad case of I-Got-This-itis.

Today is the day to say no more to "I got this!" Today is the day to lay self aside and do some serious soul searching. As God shows you where your I-Got-This-itis comes from, ask God to forgive you, and then ask the Spirit of the living God to fall afresh on you.

The late Presbyterian minister Daniel Iverson (1890–1977) wrote the song "Spirit of the Living God," the chorus of which is one of the most widely used choruses in Christian worship. It goes like this:

"Spirit of the living God, fall afresh on me. Melt me, mold me, fill me, use me. Spirit of the living God, fall afresh on me."

With Each New Assignment, You Can Ask God for Reassurance

You can sing "Spirit of the Living God, fall afresh on me" today, and be right back in your I-Got-This-itis tomorrow morning. You can stay at your daddy's house, still celebrating, tearing down the idol god altar from two years ago, but God has more for you to do. You just need to be sure that God is the one guiding you. Therefore, God gives you another life lesson from Gideon. With each new assignment, you can ask God for reassurance.

> Then Gideon said to God, "If You will deliver Israel through me, as You have spoken, behold, I will put a fleece of wool on the threshing floor. If there is dew on the fleece only, and it is dry on all the ground, then I will know that You will deliver Israel through me, as You have spoken. And it was so. When he arose early the next morning and squeezed the fleece, he drained the dew from the fleece, a bowl full of water. Then Gideon said to God, "Do not let Your anger burn against me that I may speak once more; please let me make a test once more with the fleece, let it now be dry only on the fleece, and let there be dew on all the ground." God did so that night; for it was dry only on the fleece, and dew was on all the ground. (Judges 6:36–40)

Before you go criticizing Gideon for not totally trusting God, and not learning a lesson from the first time he asked God for a sign, pay attention to what actually happened. The first thing that jumps off the page is Gideon's reassurance was connected to his calling. God, "If You will deliver Israel through me, as You have spoken" show me a sign with this fleece (verse 36). Fleece is the wool of a sheep, "whether shorn off or still attached to the skin" (Deuteronomy 18:4; Job 31:20).[5]

What did Gideon want by asking God for a sign with the fleece of a sheep? Gideon wanted to see God's hand; he wanted to be sure. Keep in mind the context in which Gideon was asking God for clarity. We get a great hint: "So Gideon said to Him, 'If now I have found favor in Your sight, then show me a sign that it is You who speak with me'" (Judges 6:17).

Why was Israel in trouble? For idol worship and doing evil in the sight of God.

What was on display where Gideon lived? The altar for the idol gods Baal and the Asherah were on display.

What did Gideon say he wanted to be sure of? "Show me a sign that it is You who speak with me" (Judges 6:17).

All I know from this context is that Israel had worshipped idol gods, and Gideon wanted to make sure that the true and living God was the one speaking to Him.

Notice what happened next: Gideon waited until the next day to see God's hand, and he reverently went deeper with God for reassurance (verse 39). Bible scholar and Christian theologian Charles Ryrie noted that Gideon realized that his first sign was not a sign at all, as the ground would have naturally dried before the fleece.[6] Therefore, Gideon, out of great respect for God, asked God not to be angry with him when he made one more request to help him to be sure. "Make the ground wet, and keep the fleece dry."

Gideon once again waited until the next day to see God's hand. What we see in Judges 6 is that Gideon had a habit of asking and waiting on God for reassurance. He was in an environment full of

---

[5] M. G. Easton, *Easton's Bible Dictionary* (New York: Harper & Brothers, 1893).
[6] Charles Ryrie, Ryrie Study Bible: expanded edition (Moody Press, 1994).

idol worship, especially at his daddy's house, and he wanted to be sure every time God gave him an assignment.

We should do the same. For each assignment that comes our way, instead of looking at it with the I-got-this mentality, we should develop the habit of asking God for reassurance.

Learn from Gideon that instead of allowing I-Got-This-itis to rush you into thoughtless actions, taking time to verify each assignment better positions us to fulfill God's call on our lives. Why step into a new assignment and then question if God called you? Be sure about each assignment, and then step out with total confidence in God as you follow the Spirit of God. Pay attention to how God honored Gideon's requests for reassurance.

Here is a personal prayer to help:

Dear heavenly Father, I thank you for your calling on my life. Lord, I desire a personal relationship with you, such that I can always be sure that you are speaking to me and giving me instructions supported in Your Word. Lord, forgive me for the times that I practiced I-Got-This-itis. I know such overconfidence in myself is not pleasing to you because I end up leaving you out and leaning on my own understanding. Father, keep me close to your bosom so that I daily depend on you. In Jesus's name, I pray. Amen.

CHAPTER 5

God Unites Our Life Callings with His Work

Judges 7

One of the great life experiences for God's children is having God unite our life callings with His work. Despite all the drama around us, God unites His call on our lives with His mighty works to restore the human race back to Him.

Look at how Jesus said this: "You did not choose Me but I chose you, and appointed you that you would go and bear fruit, and that your fruit would remain, so that whatever you ask of the Father in My name He may give to you" (John 15:16).

Look at how God said this: "Therefore, we are ambassadors for Christ, as though God were making an appeal through us; we beg you on behalf of Christ, be reconciled to God" (2 Corinthians 5:20).

The children of Israel dealt with long-term consequences for not obeying God as they conquered the Promised Land. God told them to destroy all the inhabitants of the land because of their wickedness. Under Joshua's leadership, they obeyed God, but after Joshua died, Israel began to compromise and let the people live.

The children of Israel also dealt with God's punishing them again for worshiping the idol gods of the people they let live when they conquered the Promised Land.

In Judges 6, we learn that Midian had oppressed the children of Israel for seven years. Israel cried out to God, and God placed a call on Gideon's life to deliver Israel from the Midianites.

Look at the setting: "Then all the Midianites and the Amalekites and the sons of the east assembled themselves; and they crossed over and camped in the valley of Jezreel" (Judges 6:33).

"Now the Midianites and the Amalekites and all the sons of the east were lying in the valley as numerous as locusts; and their camels were without number, as numerous as the sand on the seashore" (Judges 7:12).

These were serious consequences for disobeying God.

Some of us today are dealing with the consequences for disobeying God. God told us not to do it, but we thought we were smarter than God was, and we did it anyway.

Do you know what I like about God? When we are in trouble with God, and we cry out to Him for help, God will have mercy on us and start a deliverance process for us.

What we learn from Israel's situation is that God delivers, and God chooses to include humans in His work to deliver humans.

God does not need us, but He does choose to use us in delivering people from the consequences of sin. Can you believe that God has entrusted to us the ministry of reconciliation? Can you believe that God uses us in a variety of ways to help fellow humans get right with Him?

How do we enjoy God's uniting our life callings with His work?

In Judges 7, we will look at Gideon's story to see how we can enjoy God's uniting our life callings with His work. When we get to Judges 7, Gideon already has received several reassurances from God regarding God's call on his life to deliver Israel from Midian.

God obviously worked miracles, and Gideon and others saw God's miracle-working power up close. Let's enjoy a front-row seat in watching God unite our life callings with His miraculous work. How do we do that? We keep I-Got-This-itis out of our hearts. Remember, I-Got-This-itis is an overconfidence in self, such that it attacks our daily dependence on God and tries to fulfill God's call on our lives by leaning on our own understanding.

God's Spirit was upon Gideon as the people gathered around him.

"Then Jerubbaal (that is, Gideon) and all the people who were with him, rose early and camped beside the spring of Harod; and the camp of Midian was on the north side of them by the hill of Moreh in the valley" (Judges 7:1).

How did a man with no influence on the nation of Israel and with zero confidence in himself get the nation of Israel's military to join him in the Valley of Jezreel to fight against the massive army of Midian and their allies?

According to Judges 6:34, the Spirit of the Lord came upon Gideon, and he blew the trumpet, and the army of Israel gathered around Gideon to fight.

What made the difference? When God's Spirit came upon Gideon, He was empowered to lead the nation of Israel.

The same thing happens to us today. The Spirit of God fills us (or takes control over our lives), and then we have divine power working inside of us and working on our behalf.

In order for the Spirit of God to take control over our lives, we must be like Gideon; we must be willing, available, and obedient servants of the Lord.

As God considered Gideon's army, God recognized how the spirit of I-Got-This-itis would interfere with his work. Therefore, God dismissed 31,700 soldiers to prevent an outbreak of I-Got-This-itis. Of the people who joined Gideon, who was willing to serve on God's terms in delivering Israel from Midian? "The LORD said to Gideon, 'The people who are with you are too many for Me to give Midian into their hands, for Israel would become boastful, saying, "My own power has delivered me." Now therefore come, proclaim in the hearing of the people, saying, "Whoever is afraid and trembling, let him return and depart from Mount Gilead"'" (Judges 7:2–3). So 22,000 people returned, but 10,000 remained

What did God see? God saw the spirit of boasting in the people. The word *boast* here means to glorify oneself, to exalt oneself, to brag. God saw the wrong spirit in the people. He saw that after He worked a miracle for them, they would declare, "I got this."

First, God eliminated the fearful. He told Gideon to tell all the soldiers who were afraid and trembling that they could go home.

God recognized that even the soldiers trembling from fear would boast as if they won the battle, instead of acknowledging Him. Hence, God dismissed them.

With only ten thousand soldiers left, God still saw the spirit of I-Got-This-itis. "Then the LORD said to Gideon, 'The people are still too many; bring them down to the water and I will test them for you there. Therefore it shall be that he of whom I say to you, "This one shall go with you," he shall go with you; but everyone of whom I say to you, "This one shall not go with you," he shall not go'" (Judges 7:4).

God continued decreasing the number of soldiers by eliminating the majority of the leftover soldiers. Look at this test in Judges:

> So he brought the people down to the water. And the LORD said to Gideon, "You shall separate everyone who laps the water with his tongue as a dog laps, as well as everyone who kneels to drink." Now the number of those who lapped, putting their hand to their mouth, was 300 men; but all the rest of the

people kneeled to drink water. The LORD said to Gideon, "I will deliver you with the 300 men who lapped and will give the Midianites into your hands; so let all the other people go, each man to his home." So the 300 men took the people's provisions and their trumpets into their hands. And Gideon sent all the other men of Israel, each to his tent, but retained the 300 men; and the camp of Midian was below him in the valley. (Judges 7:5–8)

God does not explain why He choose the three hundred who lapped like a dog versus those who knelt down. All we know is God decided to deliver Israel with just three hundred soldiers.

Did you see this? When God looked at the people gathered to fight with Gideon, He ended up dismissing 31,700 soldiers to prevent an outbreak of I-Got-This-itis. God had to work a God-sized miracle to defeat Midian and all their allies as He promised.

We can easily get lost in the story of Gideon and miss what God is teaching us today. God promised to touch people, heal people, and deliver people, and He chose to use us to participate in His plan. What God promises to do requires a miracle. The question is, will we believe God for the miracle needed to serve Him?

How can you ensure that God includes you in the three hundred who see His miraculous work up close instead of from a distance? Keep I-Got-This-itis out of your heart!

God knows your heart. He knows if He can trust you. God knows if you are going to try to take credit for the miracles He works. God knows if you are thinking in your heart, "I got this." Therefore, keep I-Got-This-itis out of your heart.

How do we enjoy God's uniting our life callings with His work? Keep alert for those intimate reassurance moments with God. "Now the same night it came about that the LORD said to him, 'Arise, go down against the camp, for I have given it into your hands'" (Judges 7:9).

God knows what we need to fulfill His call on our lives.

Put yourself in Gideon's shoes—God calls you to deliver your country from a nation that is mean and cruel, and they gather allies, and camp in your land to destroy you. God promises that He will use you to deliver your nation. The Spirit of God comes on you, and you call the army, and thirty-two thousand soldiers come together to fight with you. Then God steps in and reduces your army down to three hundred soldiers.

What would you need from God at that point?

God knows what you need to fulfill the call He has on your life. Therefore, God will set up intimate moments, just when you need Him to speak to your heart and reassure you. No matter what things look like right now, and no matter how you feel, God will reassure you. God will keep His promises, but He does so in His own time and in His own way.

God knew about Gideon's need to be reassured; therefore, God met with Gideon again to reassure him. What did God tell Gideon? "Arise, go down against the camp, for I have given it into your hands" (Judges 7:9). Yes, God reassured Gideon at least four times in Judges 6, but in Judges 7, God cut his army down to three hundred, and God knew Gideon needed more reassurance. God met Gideon at night, when things were quiet and while his mind might have been racing and wondering what he was to do with only three hundred soldiers.

God used a trusted friend to help Gideon overcome fear. "But if you are afraid to go down, go with Purah your servant down to the camp" (Judges 7:10). How in the world was one man supposed to remove Gideon's fear of a multitude of fierce and cruel fighters?

Up to that point, God dealt with Gideon directly. Later, God introduced a trusted friend into Gideon's need for reassurance. He told Gideon, "If you are dealing with fear, take your friend, and go down to the enemy's camp so that I can show you that I keep my promises."

Look at Judges 7:11. "'And you will hear what they say; and afterward your hands will be strengthened that you may go down against the camp.' So he went with Purah his servant down to the outposts of the army that was in the camp."

What did God want Gideon to see or hear this time? He wanted Gideon to hear what the enemy was thinking. Therefore, God promised Gideon insights into the enemy's thinking.

"Once you hear what the enemy is saying," God told Gideon, "you will have strength to go against that massive army with just three hundred soldiers."

As God includes us in His work, He will show us several miracles leading up to the upcoming mighty miracle. God uses various personal and intimate experiences with Him to help us go deeper in our level of trust in Him.

God showed Gideon the fear He put into the hearts of a multitude of fierce enemy soldiers, not for Gideon to catch I-Got-This-itis but to build Gideon's confidence. What happened next in the story?

> When Gideon came, behold, a man was relating a dream to his friend. And he said, "Behold, I had a dream; a loaf of barley bread was tumbling into the camp of Midian, and it came to the tent and struck it so that it fell, and turned it upside down so that the tent lay flat." His friend replied, "This is nothing less than the sword of Gideon the son of Joash, a man of Israel; God has given Midian and all the camp into

his hand." When Gideon heard the account of the dream and its interpretation, he bowed in worship. He returned to the camp of Israel and said, "Arise, for the LORD has given the camp of Midian into your hands." (Judges 7:13–15)

God is always in control of our enemies. The enemy can plot and plan behind closed doors and even go to the extreme, as the Midianites and their allies did by spreading out over the valley of Jezreel. They can plan to get us in strategic places to hurt us the deepest, but God is always in control of our enemies.

Here, thousands and thousands of the Midianites and their allies spread all over the valley, but they were terrified. When thousands and thousands of fierce warriors, who outnumber and can overpower their opponents, know that they are going to lose the battle, then who is really in control? God is. What did God tell Gideon? "Surely I will be with you, and you shall defeat Midian as one man" (Judges 6:16).

When God calls an intimate meeting with you, respond with worship. God called Gideon to an intimate meeting. It was as if God said, "Gideon, let me show you how I am working before the battle starts." As gospel music songwriter Donald Lawrence put it in "When the Battle Is Over,"

Don't wait till the battle is over, shout now,

You know in the end you're gonna win.

Gideon was greatly encouraged. Having a little intimate time with God, just you and God alone, will encourage your heart, despite your circumstances.

What did Gideon do when God showed him the dream and its interpretation in verse 15? Gideon bowed before the Lord and worshipped. Gideon got his shout on! He stopped to recognize the true and living God, and he stopped and praised the Lord.

You'd better learn how to stop and let God encourage your heart in the midst of your sickness, your tragedy, the attack on your family, the uncertainty—stop! God will schedule an intimate meeting with you.

Your responsibility is to get to the meeting so that God can encourage your heart. The next thing to do is stop and worship God in the middle of the crisis, in the middle of the enemy's plotting and planning, in the middle of the enemy's trying to turn you every which way but loose.

Respond to God's intimate meeting to reassure you with worship. After worship, respond with faith-based action.

God is not a hold-your-head-down-in-defeat type of God! God is not the complaining type! God is not a leave-His-children-depressed-and-oppressed God. God is the God of victory! God is the God who keeps His promise.

After Gideon worshipped God, what did he do next? He responded with faith-based action. He went back to God's super-powered army of only three hundred solders, and cried out, "Arise! The Lord has given us the victory. Let's go!"

Don't just sit there. Give the battle cry. Charge! Respond to God with faith-based action.

God will encourage you in the middle of your crisis, but you must keep alert for the intimate meeting that God wants to have with you so that He can reassure you of the promises He made to you.

Allow God to Do the Impossible through You (Judges 7:16–25)

How do you enjoy God uniting your life calling with His work? Allow God to do the impossible through you. Confidently lead people to do the impossible with God's name on it.

> He divided the 300 men into three companies, and
> he put trumpets and empty pitchers into the hands
> of all of them, with torches inside the pitchers. He
> said to them, "Look at me and do likewise. And
> behold, when I come to the outskirts of the camp, do
> as I do. "When I and all who are with me blow the
> trumpet, then you also blow the trumpets all around
> the camp and say, 'For the LORD and for Gideon.'"
> (Judges 7:16–18)

As Gideon confidently led the people to do the impossible, what
did he do? He put God's name on the victory.

I especially appreciate Gideon right here because this was a
perfect time for I-Got-This-itis to show up and mess up everything.
Overconfidence could have overcome Gideon, and he could have
forgot about all the miracles that God worked to get him to the edge
of victory, but Gideon put God's name on this battle call: "For the
LORD and for Gideon!"

When God trusts you, God connects you to His mighty works
(Judges 7:18; cf. John 15:16). Keep the order straight: "For the
LORD and for Gideon."

Wait a minute—why was Gideon's name included in the battle
cry? 'Wasn't Gideon supposed to stay out of the battle call? When
God trusts you, God connects you to His mighty works. God clearly
confronted the enemy and put fear in their hearts, but God dropped
Gideon's name in the mix. Do you remember what Gideon heard
one of the enemy soldiers say when he went on the spying mission?
"I had a dream; a loaf of barley bread was tumbling into the camp
of Midian, and it came to the tent and stuck it so that it fell, and
turned it upside down so that the tent lay flat." His friend answered,
"This is nothing less than the sword of Gideon the son of Joash, a

man of Israel; God, has given Midian and all the camp into his hand" (Judges 7:13–14).

God, not Gideon, was going to destroy them and give them into the hand of Gideon.

God was the one who dropped Gideon's name in the mix. God did all the work, but He associated Gideon's name with the victory.

If God did all the heavy lifting, why did he mention Gideon's name in the victory call?

God could not trust those other 31,700 soldiers, but God trusted Gideon and three hundred soldiers to keep things straight. Gideon said, "For the Lord and for Gideon."

When God trusts you like this and connects you to His mighty works, keep the order straight. Not for Gideon and for the Lord, but "for the Lord and for Gideon."

Can you imagine confronting a huge army with three hundred soldiers armed with trumpets, pitchers, torches, and a war cry ("For the Lord, and for Gideon")?

> So Gideon and the hundred men who were with him came to the outskirts of the camp at the beginning of the middle watch, when they had just posted the watch; and they blew the trumpets and smashed the pitchers that were in their hands. When the three companies blew the trumpets and broke the pitchers, they held the torches in their left hands and the trumpets in their right hands for blowing, and cried, "A sword for the LORD and for Gideon!" Each stood in his place around the camp; and all the army ran, crying out as they fled. When they blew 300 trumpets, the LORD set the sword of one against another even throughout the whole army; and the

army fled as far as Beth-shittah toward Zererah, as far as the edge of Abel-meholah, by Tabbath. (Judges 7:19–22)

Where's the sense in confronting a huge army with three hundred soldiers armed with trumpets, pitchers, torches, and a war cry? To the human mind, this action makes zero sense. For a child of God, however, who has the Spirit of God upon him and reassurance after reassurance from God, God's way is the only way that makes sense.

You don't have to imagine how unreal God's plans are, just take what God has given you, and move forward with faith-based action. The battle is the Lord's, and He simply connects you with the victory. "For the Lord and for Gideon!"

God will bring the other people back in to help but in a way they can only help and not take credit for a God-sized miracle (verses 23–25).

Aren't you glad that God is not like us? Would you have left the 31,700 soldiers—those that God initially dismissed from the heart of the battle—completely out of the action? God is not like us. Despite their severe case of I-Got-This-itis that got them dismissed from the battle, God saw fit to bring them back into the action—but in a way that they could only help but not take credit for the God-sized miracle that occurred.

The men of Israel were summoned from Naphtali and Asher and all Manasseh, and they pursued Midian. Gideon sent messengers throughout all the hill country of Ephraim, saying, "Come down against Midian and take the waters before them, as far as Beth-barah and the Jordan." So all the men of

Ephraim were summoned and they took the waters as far as Beth-barah and the Jordan. They captured the two leaders of Midian, Oreb and Zeeb, and they killed Oreb at the rock of Oreb, and they killed Zeeb at the wine press of Zeeb, while they pursued Midian; and they brought the heads of Oreb and Zeeb to Gideon from across the Jordan. (Judges 7:23–25)

Gideon could have complained to God. He might have said, "God, why should we bring them in at this point? We don't need them. We did all this by ourselves."

I really appreciate Gideon for staying focused, out of God's business, and for doing what the Spirit of God led him to do.

The key point here is allow God to do the impossible through you. Your job is not to dictate to God on how to do things. Your job is to simply allow God to do the impossible through you. Stay focused on what God is doing. Avoid being caught up in how God chooses to use other people because that is not your business. Simply stay willing and available to God, so that God's Spirit will be upon you, and God will use you to lead people into doing the impossible.

This is how you enjoy God's uniting your life calling into His work. You keep I-Got-This-itis out of your heart. Keep alert for those intimate reassurance moments with God, and allow God to do the impossible through you.

Here is a personal prayer to help:

Lord, throughout the Bible You display a pattern of calling your children to do a job, and you end up doing the heavy lifting with your mighty works. Lord, I desire to be your available and willing servant, as Gideon was. I desire to live out my calling without I-Got-This-itis. I desire to have those special intimate meetings with you, and I desire to enjoy your doing the impossible in and through me. "Spirit of the living God, fall afresh on me, Melt me, mold me, fill me, use me. Spirit of the living God, fall afresh on me." In the name of Jesus, the Son of the living God, I pray. Amen.

CHAPTER 6

When God Drops the Unusual into Your Lap

Judges 13:1–23

As we study the Bible, we learn that God reaches into time and picks out ordinary people to participate in His eternal plan to restore humanity back to Him.

For instance, God dropped the unusual in the laps of Mary and Joseph, who had already completed the contractual phase of the Jewish wedding ceremony, when Mary came up pregnant. In phase one of the Jewish wedding ceremony, the couple enters into a legally binding contract, and they are 100 percent married. In phase two, after the bride's family receives the payment for her (dowry), the groom comes to the bride's father's house at a time established by the bride's father and the groom, and he and the bride come together for that special time designed for married couples.

Phase three is the celebration, where the groom takes his bride from her father's house to his home, which could be on his family's property.

Mary and Joseph were in phase one when God dropped the unusual assignment for them to give birth to and parent the Christ child, the Son of the living God.

Even today, God chooses to use us to do good works and participate with Him. We share the good news about Jesus with nonbelievers, and we help the poor, the widows, and the orphans. We build hospitals, schools, wells, and churches; we help when tragedy strikes, and so on.

God often drops the unusual in our laps. He does not always ask us to do simple things that are easy and that bring popularity to our lives.

Sometimes God asks us to do things, based on His Word, that cause people to dislike us.

Sometimes God asks us to say things from His Word that are not popular.

Sometimes God asks us to make ethical decisions on our jobs that hold people accountable and maintain the standard, when others want to break the rules for selfish motives.

Sometimes God asks us to take a leadership role that requires dedication, extra sacrifice, and commitment to others.

Sometimes we want to do one thing, but God calls us in a different direction.

Sometimes God calls us to lead, and sometimes God calls us to follow.

The reality is that when we give our hearts to Jesus, God gives us spiritual gifts that fit our personalities and learning styles, and we do not have any input. Then God calls us to do things in the area of our spiritual gifts that may not always be comfortable for us, but because we love and trust God, we submit to what God is doing in and through our lives.

Do you want to be happy and enjoy fulfillment in your life here on earth? Through prayer and studying God's Word, and through interacting with godly people, you can find out what God is doing and how God wants to use you in what He is doing. Get on God's team doing what God has called you to do in connection with what He is doing.

In Judges 13, God dropped the unusual in the laps of two ordinary people who were minding their own business and simply doing life.

The setting is when the children of Israel were in the Promised Land. Because they did not follow God's instructions as they conquered the Promised Land, they were dealing with the consequences for disobeying God. The children of Israel were in trouble with God again because God caught them worshipping the idol gods of the people God told them to destroy. As their consequence, the Philistines oppressed the children of Israel forty years. This time we do not read that the children of Israel cried out. Actually, we see God's challenge to Israel in Judges 10:13-14, where God told them He was tired of their falling back into the same old sin of worshipping idol gods. God told them He would no longer deliver them, and then God told them go call on the idol gods they worshipped and to let their idol gods deliver them. Well, Israel put away their idols and started doing right, and God could not stand to see them suffer any longer (Judges 10:16). God raised up a deliverer to help them through that spiritual and physical crisis.

"Now the sons of Israel again did evil in the sight of the LORD, so that the LORD gave them into the hands of the Philistines forty years" (Judges 13:1).

What should you do when God drops the unusual into your lap?

The backdrop for our calling today is very similar to the backdrop in Judges 13. In our current society, we are in trouble—running after idol gods, practicing immorality, and doing our own thing and leaving God out. This is an old trend among humans. What should you do to get right and turn back to God when God drops the unusual into your lap?

The first thing you should do when God drops the unusual into your lap is to recognize that God is in control of the unusual.

A barren woman having a child is unusual. "There was a certain man of Zorah, of the family of the Danites, whose name was Manoah; and his wife was barren and had borne no children. Then the angel of the LORD appeared to the woman and said to her, 'Behold now, you are barren and have borne no children, but you shall conceive and give birth to a son'" (Judges 13:2–3).

Our immediate attention is not on the man of Zorah named Manoah. Our attention jumps to the barren woman. Although her name is not given, we cannot help but notice her. Why? Because a barren woman having a child is unusual. The word barren refers to a woman who cannot physically bear children. Yet in this passage, God picked out a barren woman to do the unusual and give birth to a child.

Have you ever noticed that people in the Bible who seem left out or left with the question of "Why me?" are not forgotten by God but get leading roles in God's program?

Barren women often struggle with the question of their value. They ask God. "Why did you take the experience of childbearing away from me?" Barren women often feel as if something is missing in their lives. Sometimes they even feel distant from other women, and they feel challenged in a country like the United States, where we kill over a million babies a year through abortion.

The Bible shows God calling on several barren women to serve in special roles throughout human history.

God chose Sarah, a barren woman, to be the mother of the nation of Israel (Genesis 21:12).

Rachael, a barren woman, gave birth to two tribes of Israel (Genesis 25:19–23). Her son Joseph was God's man in Egypt (Genesis 41:39–46).

Hannah, a barren woman, became the mother of the great prophet Samuel (1 Samuel 1:19–20).

Elizabeth, a barren woman, gave birth to John the Baptist (Luke 1:5–25; 57–60).

You, God's woman, who just happen to be barren in this life, are not left out. God's special calling is upon your life.

Although you might feel that God has forgotten about you, God already had you in mind before you were born. He made you fearfully and wonderfully (Psalm 139:14–18), and He has a purpose for your life (Ephesians 2:10).

Your role may not be the same as the women in the Bible just mentioned, but rest assured that God has a specific role for you. God is the one who dropped the unusual into your lap, and God is the one in control of your unusual.

When God drops the unusual into your lap, it doesn't matter where you're from or what you're going through. What does matter is that God's unusual usually comes with instructions.

"Now therefore, be careful not to drink wine or strong drink, nor eat any unclean thing. For behold, you shall conceive and give birth to a son, and no razor shall come upon his head, for the boy shall be a Nazirite to God from the womb; and he shall begin to deliver Israel from the hands of the Philistines" (Judges 13:4–5).

The barren woman received direct instructions in the above verses. She could not drink wine or strong drinks. She could not eat forbidden foods (bacon; ham; pork ribs; ham hocks; pickled pig's feet, ears, and lips; or other forms of pork; catfish; lobster; crab; crayfish; shark meat; rabbits; or squirrels (see the forbidden foods list in Leviticus 11).

The barren woman also received direct instructions for her unborn son—he should not cut his hair ("no razor shall come upon his head"), and she was to raise him as a Nazirite from birth.

Easton's Bible Dictionary indicates that the word *Nazirite* generally denotes one who is separated from others and consecrated to God.

The vow of a Nazirite involved these three things: (1) abstinence from wine and strong drink, (2) refraining from cutting the hair off the head during the whole period of the Nazirite vow, and (3) avoidance of contact with the dead.[7] (You can see these details in Numbers 6:2–21. In the case of Samson, God said he would be a Nazirite for his entire life.)

The barren women in the above verses needed to realize that she was raising a deliverer for Israel. In this case, God was raising up a deliverer who would begin to deliver Israel from the Philistines. They would not get total deliverance, but God put in place the beginning of their deliverance. The barren woman and her husband had to raise their son and teach him his God-given role.

God shows us that we are not in control of His call on our lives. God sets the standards for how He chooses to use us.

God thrust the barren women into awesome responsibility. Her diet immediately changed. Her body would go through radical change during pregnancy, and her years of joy, heartaches, personal sacrifices, nurturing, and training as a mother were about to kick in.

God's "unusual" is not unusual in scripture—think of Gideon, Joshua, Mary and Joseph, and so on. God just comes into our lives with His unusual and turns our world upside down. Look at a few examples:

- Gideon's unusual was that he would tear down his father's idol god altar, establish a new one, and deliver Israel from Midian oppression.
- Joshua's unusual would be that he would lead Israel across the Jordan River.

---

[7] M. G. Easton, *Easton's Bible Dictionary* (New York: Harper & Brothers, 1893).

- Joshua's unusual would be that he would circumcise all the men, including the military, and leave the entire nation vulnerable to enemy attack in the open plains of Jericho.

- Joshua's unusual was to conquer Jericho by marching around Jericho in worship, when the enemy could have easily attacked them.

- Mary and Joseph's unusual was giving birth to the Savior of the world (Mary was a virgin who became pregnant, and Joseph had to stay with Mary, who was pregnant after the Holy Spirit put God inside of her).

- One of our unusual instructions from God is to live in a culture full of compromise and not allow the culture to change us (Romans 12:1–2).

- Another unusual from God is for us to tell people the story of how God sent His Son into the world to die for our sins and get us right with Him. The story does not make sense from a human perspective, but the story contains the power of God to change people's lives (Romans 1:16).

God's unusual way of stepping into your world and including you in His eternal plan to restore humankind back to Him is unusual. As God drops the unusual into your lap, recognize that God is dealing with you, and submit to His call on your life.

Get The Right Prayer Partners Involved (Judges 13:6–14)

When God drops the unusual into your lap, get the right prayer partners. In all the years that I have read this story, I missed the picture of the powerful prayer partners in Judges 13.

Who were the prayer partners in Judges 13? The barren woman and her husband, Manoah, were the prayer partners. Watch the flow of this powerful husband-and-wife prayer partnership.

> Then the woman came and told her husband, saying, "A man of God came to me and his appearance was like the appearance of the angel of God, very awesome. And I did not ask him where he came from, nor did he tell me his name. But he said to me, 'Behold, you shall conceive and give birth to a son, and now you shall not drink wine or strong drink nor eat any unclean thing, for the boy shall be a Nazirite to God from the womb to the day of his death.'" (Judges 13:6–7)

What was the first thing the wife did after she had an encounter with the angel of the Lord? She shared the unusual with her husband. The barren woman did not call her mother. She did not call her siblings or friends first; she went to her husband. This husband and wife apparently had a close prayer-based relationship. Notice that the woman did not keep the information that would change her home to herself because she clearly trusted her husband as a godly man. She trusted his judgment, and she trusted his leadership over their home. She shared all the details, and her husband carefully listened because he was a godly man who was responsible for his household.

Do you notice positive characteristics in Manoah? He was approachable, and he listened to his wife. Instead of panicking, Manoah immediately went to God in prayer. "Then Manoah entreated the LORD and said, 'O Lord, please let the man of God whom You have sent come to us again that he may teach us what to do for the boy who is to be born'" (Judges 13:8).

Nice to see a man take the spiritual leadership over his family. What did Manoah do? Did he accuse his wife of imagining things and being out of touch with reality? Did he complain about the upcoming changes in their life? No, he immediately went to God in prayer. "O Lord, please bring the man of God back to us so that he can teach us what to do for the boy."

Manoah's prayer focused on God's will for his family. God put the unusual in Manoah's lap, and Manoah went straight to God to learn how to parent their unusual son.

Notice that Manoah's prayer was not about what he and his wife would get. He was not trying to cut a deal with God to share in the fame of his upcoming superhero son. Manoah's prayer was concentrated on God's will. "God, what role do you want my wife and me to play in this child's life?" he might have asked. "We know You will take him for Your service all of his life, so tell us how we should raise the boy. What should we teach him? What should we do for him?" Instead of taking matters into their own hands, they quickly sought direction from God.

> God listened to the voice of Manoah; and the angel of God came again to the woman as she was sitting in the field, but Manoah her husband was not with her. So the woman ran quickly and told her husband, "Behold, the man who came the other day has appeared to me." Then Manoah arose and followed his wife, and when he came to the man he said to him, "Are you the man who spoke to the woman?" And he said, "I am." (Judges 13:9–11)

I love this couple. The angel of the Lord returned to Manoah's wife while Manoah was absent. Manoah's wife quickly ran to get her husband. Notice that Manoah did not question his wife or doubt her. He quickly followed her so that he could get the answer to his prayer.

Manoah asked the angel of the Lord for clarification regarding their son. In verse 12, Manoah said, "Now when your words come to pass, what shall be the boy's mode of life and his vocation?"

Notice the faith of Manoah and his wife. They never doubted that they would have a baby, nor did they question God on how such a miracle could ever happen. They simply started living in their miracle. The boy was not born yet, but they started living as if the boy was born and able to learn. "Lord, tell us, what is the boy going to do? What will his job be?"

The Nazirite vow was clear. As Manoah and his wife listened to the angel of the Lord, notice that God repeated His previous instructions and put emphasis on the woman keeping herself dedicated to God.

"So the angel of the LORD said to Manoah, 'Let the woman pay attention to all that I said. She should not eat anything that comes from the vine nor drink wine or strong drink, nor eat any unclean thing; let her observe all that I commanded'" (Judges 13:13–14).

God's unusual may overwhelm you if you do not pray. Manoah and his wife settled into the reality of not having children, but God decided to drop the unusual into their laps. When God drops the unusual into your lap, pray for the right prayer partners, share the information with them, pray together, and carefully listen to God's answer to your prayer.

Stop moving so fast and pray. Stop jumping in and asking questions later. Stop and pray. Get the right prayer partners, and pray together. Hear from God and continue to seek God's clear directions.

Brothers, do you lead your wives in prayer each day? Do you listen to your wives, such that when the unusual happens with your wives, they will come to you because they trust you as godly men who will immediately go to God in prayer?

Regardless of your marital status, we, as believers, need to be around godly people who pray. Be intentional in taking time to pray. Get closer to God through your time of prayer. Let God soften and sensitize your heart. Get off the fast track, and take more time to pray. The hustle and bustle of life and the "what do I do next?" mentality is killing our spiritual growth.

Many of us are coming to church, looking for direction on how to grow in the midst of extremely busy lives, but we have not put in any personal prayer time.

If you do not have a prayer partner, ask God to give you the right person(s).

Husbands and wives, you are prayer partners. Stop all the excuses, and make time to pray together each day. You can have other prayer partners, but your spouse is to be your primary prayer partner.

Here is a personal prayer to help:

Dear Lord, sometimes your plan for me is what I consider unusual. Lord, as I end this day and began a new day, I recognize you as my Lord, who can drop your unusual plan in my lap without my permission. Lord, when you give me one of your unusual assignments, help me to recognize your work in my life, give me the right prayer partners, and instead of panicking, running in fear, or trying to alter your plan, help me to respond to my encounter with you in worship and total obedience. I love you. Amen.

CHAPTER 7

More Insight on When God Drops the Unusual into Your Lap

Judges 13:1–23

God has already dropped the unusual in your lap. Unusual situations already occurred in your life. For instance, your salvation experience is unusual. Humans do not automatically give up operating independently to submit to God. To live a life separated from our obsession with ourselves, the worship of money and things, and practicing wicked behavior is what God does inside of us. Something outside of the human realm must happen inside the human spirit to cause us to turn to God, give up selfish pursuits, and live for God (Philippians 2:13).

Here is another unusual that God has already dropped into our laps: humans cannot get rid of their guilt and shame by doing good works. God does not accept human works as payment for our sins. God only accepts the blood of Jesus to pay for our sins and to remove the guilt and the shame that comes with sin (Ephesians 2:8–9).

God dropped the unusual into our laps just by the process of our being Christians. Now we have new identities. Now we represent

God in a culture that doesn't want the values taught in God's Word, the Bible (2 Corinthians 5:17–21).

We have gained insight from Judges 13 regarding God's calling Samson's mother, a barren women, to do the unusual and give birth to a son, who would deliver Israel from the Philistines. From that scene in Judges 13, I raised the question, what should you do when God drops the unusual into your lap? What do you do when God asks you to do something that is just not normal, or He puts a total surprise in your lap?

The doctor says you have cancer, but God still has you on assignment.

Your bank account is low, but God tells you to give a little extra money.

Everybody is on pins and needles and doesn't know what to say, but God tells you to declare the hope that we have in Christ.

Everybody in the room is drinking alcohol and doing weed or other drugs, but God tells you, "You'd better not touch it, and you'd better be a witness for me." God tells you to stand up, stand out, and stand above the drinking and the drugs so that when your friends crash in life, you will still have your credibility, your good name, and your mind, and you can lead them out of darkness and into the light in Christ (1 Corinthians 9:27).

What should you do when God drops the unusual in your lap? You already have learned two responses:

Recognize that God is in control of the unusual (Judges 13:2–5).

Get the right prayer partners involved (Judges 13:6–14).

Here's another insight from the book of Judges:

> When God drops the unusual into your lap, let your
> encounter with God lead to worship of God (Judges
> 13:15–23).

Worship is recognizing and revering God because of who He is,
what He has done, what He is doing, and what He is going to do.

God answered Manoah's prayer in Judges 13, and the angel of the
Lord reappeared to Manoah and his wife, restating that she would
have a baby, that the baby would be a Nazirite from his birth until
his death, and that his wife must change her diet and practices to
reflect the Nazirite vow of no wine or other alcoholic beverages and
no unclean food.

This gives encouragement to those women who are with child—
eat right and do right while you are carrying a baby; you are carrying
a child who belongs to God.

After the angel put special emphasis on the barren woman's eating
right and doing right, look at what happened next:

"Then Manoah said to the angel of the LORD, 'Please let us
detain you so that we may prepare a young goat for you.' The angel
of the LORD said to Manoah, 'Though you detain me, I will not
eat your food, but if you prepare a burnt offering, then offer it to
the LORD.' For Manoah did not know that he was the angel of the
LORD" (Judges 13:15–16).

To Manoah, the angel of the Lord was a stranger, and according
to Near Eastern customs at that time, Manoah showed kindness by
offering food to the angel of the Lord.

Most of us would not turn down good food, but the angel of
the Lord did, saying, "I will stay with you for a few days, but I will
not eat your food. What you can do is focus your thanksgiving and

refocus your energy, time, and efforts to honoring the Lord. What you can do is take the young goat you were going to cook for me and offer it as a burnt offering to the Lord."

We learn about the burnt offering in Leviticus 1:1–17 and 6:8–13. The book *Manners and Customs of the Bible* describes a burnt offering as a symbol of entire and perpetual consecration to God. People who gave burnt offerings had their sins forgiven by God, were cleansed to serve God, and were to continually dedicate themselves to God.[8]

The fire from the burnt offering never went out. The smoke from the offering went up to God throughout the day and was a soothing aroma to God.

Manoah did not recognize the presence of God at this point, although we don't know why he did not recognize the Lord. Perhaps the culture in which he lived influenced him. Israel's spiritual condition was low. They were in a forty-year punishment from God because of idol worship.

We do know that God was patient with Manoah and his wife. By having Manoah go beyond cooking a dinner to offering a burnt offering, God directed Manoah to recognize His presence.

Israel was dirty and busy worshipping idol gods, and God was spanking them, but God set Manoah and his wife apart to bring in a deliverer for Israel. They needed to consecrate themselves; they needed to give the burnt offering to have their sins forgiven and to symbolize their commitment to dedicating themselves to the unusual call on their lives.

How sensitive are you in recognizing the presence of God in the midst of your unusual? God constantly tries to get our attention, and get us to dedicate ourselves to His call on our lives. Try not to focus

---

[8] James M. Freeman and Harold J. Chadwick, *Manners & Customs of the Bible* (North Brunswick, NJ: Bridge-Logos Publishers, 1998), 145.

so much on the circumstances surrounding your unusual, and offer yourself as a living sacrifice unto God.

The redirection of Manoah—from spending his time and energy trying to feed God to simply recognizing God and worshiping Him—is a powerful lesson for us. We cannot meet God's needs because God is not a stranger in town with no place to go or eat. We do not need to take God into our lives to help God; we need to receive God into our lives because He has the plan for our lives, and we need Him to help us.

Jesus was our burnt offering when He died on the cross. When Jesus offered Himself as the burnt offering, He dealt with our sins. God forgave our sins, and God expects dedication to Him.

This is the heart of Romans 12:1, where God tells us to offer ourselves as living sacrifices. This is where we make up our minds and offer ourselves to God once for all. This is a long-lasting, lifelong sacrifice. We never stop in our dedicated life to God.

Instead of cooking a dinner, the angel of the Lord instructed Manoah to offer a sacrifice to the Lord. Who was this person rejecting customary hospitality? What was his name?

Manoah said to the angel of the LORD, 'What is your name, so that when your words come to pass, we may honor you?' But the angel of the LORD said to him, 'Why do you ask my name, seeing it is wonderful?'" (Judges 13:17–18).

Instead of giving honor in what Manoah thought was a human situation, God led Manoah to reflect on the incomprehensible. "Why do you ask my name, seeing it is wonderful?" According to the *Theological Wordbook of the Old Testament*, the word wonderful refers to God and the acts of God, both of which are incomprehensible and beyond human capabilities.

The incomprehensibleness of God brings awakening and astonishment to humankind.

The astonishment, the wake-up, is not the fact that a miracle occurred but that God forcibly struck an impression in the human mind that He exists, that He cares, that no one is like Him, and that only He can do what was just done.[9] God uses miracles so that we can see Him, not just the miracle.

It is as if He said, "Why do you want to know my name, being that my name is wonderful, incomprehensible, and constantly working to astonish, to wake up the human consciousness about God?" Even after the angel of the Lord told Manoah that he could not understand the greatness of His name, Manoah still did not recognize the presence of God.

Can you think of a time when you just missed God's presence? While caught up in your unusual situation, you did not recognize God's hand.

You cannot explain why you were in your situation. All you know is that your life took an unusual twist. The unexpected hit you, and you needed supernatural help.

Do you remember a time when you panicked and responded to your situation with your human resources and just missed seeing or seeking the hand of God?

God gave us this lesson in Judges 13 to teach us how easy it is to miss the hand of God dropping the unusual in our laps.

God wants us to learn how to be still and know that He is God, He will be exalted among the heathens, He will be exalted in the earth—"the Lord of host is with us; the God of Jacob is our refuge" (Psalm 46:11 KJV). We can run to God and safely rest.

God's divine display led Manoah and his wife to worship (Judges 13:19–20).

---

[9] Victor P. Hamilton, "1768 אָלַף," ed. R. Laird Harris, Gleason L. Archer Jr., and Bruce K. Waltke, *Theological Wordbook of the Old Testament* (Chicago: Moody Press, 1999), 723.

So the angel of the Lord told Manoah to take the young goat he was about to cook for a dinner and offer it as a burnt offering to the Lord. Look at what happened next:

"So Manoah took the young goat with the grain offering and offered it on the rock to the LORD, and He performed wonders while Manoah and his wife looked on. For it came about when the flame went up from the altar toward heaven, that the angel of the LORD ascended in the flame of the altar. When Manoah and his wife saw this, they fell on their faces to the ground" (Judges 13:19–20).

Notice that Manoah added a grain offering to the burnt offering, which was to express his and his wife's thankful hearts and their dedication to God. God's response was to perform wonders while Manoah and his wife looked on.

The word *wonders* is consistent with what the angel of the Lord said about His name. Right in the presence of Manoah and his wife, God worked a miracle that forcible astonished Manoah and his wife. Then the angel of the Lord did what only God could do—He went up, and He left the scene through the altar flame.

This was an "only God" moment. Only God could do such a thing. The person who introduced the unusual of a barren woman having a baby—something humanly impossible—was God.

The person who gave clear direction for the unusual situation was God.

The person who was the answer to Manoah's prayer was God.

The person who came back and directed Manoah to offer a burnt offering was God.

The person who could have left Manoah and his wife wondering but patiently explained how to deal with their unusual son and then worked wonders in front of them was God.

Surely, Manoah and his wife saw God as wonderful because they could not deny what they had experienced.

What is the human response when God displays His wonders to behold? We fall on our faces and worship Him.

Here are a couple of nuggets to take away from this ancient story:

- Don't just see the wonders but also see the wonder of God's patient and personal touch in the human realm.
- God wants us to understand His unusual, His unusual instructions, and His commitment to help His children participate in His eternal plan.

One of the last things Satan wants us to do is worship God. Satan wants us to remain preoccupied with ourselves. He wants us to use good deeds to rid ourselves of guilt and shame. Satan does not want us to forget about ourselves and concentrate on God (or concentrate on whom God is, what God has done, what He is doing, and what His is going to do).

Why is Satan determined to keep us from worshipping God? Satan cannot keep us in confusion when we are worshipping God.

Satan cannot keep our eyes blinded to the wonders of God when we continually seek God because when we seek God, we will find God and see His wonders, and we will worship God.

Satan cannot stop us from dedicating ourselves to God as a living and holy sacrifice when we worship God.

Where did these principles come from? Notice what happened after the angel of the Lord left. "Now the angel of the LORD did not appear to Manoah or his wife again. Then Manoah knew that he was the angel of the LORD. So Manoah said to his wife, 'We will surely die, for we have seen God.' But his wife said to him, 'If the LORD had desired to kill us, He would not have accepted a burnt offering and a grain offering from our hands, nor would He have shown us all these things, nor would He have let us hear things like this at this time'" (Judges 13:21–23).

Satan tried to kill this couple's future hope. Manoah, the prayer warrior, recognized that the angel of the Lord was God Himself, and his mind immediately went to Exodus 33:20, where God said, "For no man can see Me and live!"

After all the hope that God gave to Manoah and his wife, Manoah thought God was going to kill them after He wonderfully revealed Himself, and they worshipped God.

God does not give hope, and then destroy the hope He gives.

Although God left their presence through the fire on the altar, God did not leave Manoah and his wife. God saw Manoah's panic, and He used Manoah's wife to bring words of assurance.

The barren woman? Manoah's wife? Have you noticed that we are not told wife's name? One great lesson on God's not revealing the name of the barren women is this: when God chooses to use us and works His wonders to confirm His desire to use us, our names, woven into God's plan and promises for our lives. God's plan for us is not to popularize our names; God's plan gives us more lasting fulfillment. What we do while working with God to help people is more fulfilling than people knowing our names.

The barren woman found herself caught in God's plan for her life. What did she do when her husband thought God was going to kill them? Did she make her husband feel bad? Did she call him a scared chicken? Did she insult him by attacking his misunderstanding of God's appearance to them? Did she attack his manhood and leadership over the home? Did she insinuate that she was smarter or better than her husband was? No, she quickly brought words of assurance to her husband.

How did she reassure her husband? Pay attention here; the barren woman simply stood on God's word that she would give birth to a future leader.

When fear attacks the hope that God gives us, God often uses a human voice to encourage us. In this case, God used the wife to encourage her husband.

I love this couple. As life has it, even people who are spiritual can make a mistake. Manoah was a praying man. When God put the unusual in their laps, Manoah led his wife in prayer to seek God's clear direction for their family. Manoah and his wife both witnessed the wonders of God in their marriage, and they both worshipped God. Now, just because he missed something that seems obvious and made a mistake about God, his wife—the barren woman, the one who wondered if she had value—did not kick her husband to the curb. Instead, she encouraged her husband based on God's promises.

Practice more often what you see in Judges 13. When you see people's hopes shattered, quickly reassure them, based on God's promises.

Here is a personal prayer to help:

Dear Lord, sometimes your plan for me is what I consider unusual. Lord, as I face each day, I recognize you as my Lord, who can drop your unusual plan in my lap without my permission. Lord, when you give me one of your unusual assignments, help me to recognize your work in my life and give me the right prayer partners. Instead of my panicking, running in fear, or trying to alter your plan, help me to respond to my encounter with you in worship and total obedience. Father, heighten my spiritual senses so that I recognize your presence and your power in my midst. I want to see and feel evidence of your presence. I want to hear your voice. Draw me close to you, and come close to me, and walk with me and talk with me along the way. I love you deeply. In the name of Jesus, I pray. Amen.

CHAPTER 8

When God's Servants Neglect to Pray

Judges 14

Every Christian is a servant of God, and we need to know what happens when we neglect to pray. Let's explore some of the outcomes.

In Judges 13, we saw a powerful example of a married couple's prayer partnership. God dropped the unusual in the laps of a barren women and her husband, Manoah. The angel of the Lord told the barren women she was going to have a baby. That baby would be a superhero and would deliver Israel from the oppression of the Philistines. The Philistines oppressed Israel for forty years because God punished Israel for their disrespectful and evil behavior.

The angel of the Lord forcible struck the minds of Manoah and his wife with the wonders of the incomprehensibleness of God, and they bowed down and worshipped God.

We learned that God does exist. He cares about us, no one is like Him, and no one can do what He does.

The book of Judges displays Israel's roller coaster relationship with God, but Judges 13 shows us that Israel still had people who were faithful in their relationship with God. Let's look at what happened next in the most spiritually charged and spiritually uplifting chapter in the entire book of Judges. "Then the woman gave birth to a son and named him Samson; and the child grew up and the LORD blessed him. And the Spirit of the LORD began to stir him in Mahaneh-dan, between Zorah and Eshtaol" (Judges 13:24–25).

God leaves us with the impression that the boy is going to learn from his godly momma and daddy and be a prayer warrior like his parents. Look at the end of verse 24: "and the child grew up and the LORD blessed him." God leaves us with the expectation that the blessed boy will be a blessing because God's blessing was upon him.

So what happens when God's servants neglect to pray?

Judges 14 opens with the painful reality that our parents can be godly prayer warriors, and we can be just the opposite if we neglect to pray.

In Judges 14, we learn that we can come out of a spiritually uplifting situation, such as in Judges 13, and end up driven by our fleshly desires and miss the fulfillment that comes from living for God.

Because of the contrast between Judges 13 and Judges 14, we raise the question: what happens when we, as God's servants, neglect to pray, neglect to seek God's direction, and do our own thing? We aimlessly wander into self-gratifying pursuits.

"Then Samson went down to Timnah and saw a woman in Timnah, one of the daughters of the Philistines" (Judges 14:1).

Samson was four to six miles away from home, aimlessly wandering. You don't need to travel far for aimless wandering; you simply need to neglect to pray. God called Samson to deliver Israel from Philistine oppression, but without prayer, Samson found himself aimlessly wandering.

While aimlessly wandering, Samson came under attack by the lust of his eyes.

"So he came back and told his father and mother, 'I saw a woman in Timnah, one of the daughters of the Philistines; now therefore, get her for me as a wife.' Then his father and his mother said to him, 'Is there no woman among the daughters of your relatives, or among all our people, that you go to take a wife from the uncircumcised Philistines?' But Samson said to his father, 'Get her for me, for she looks good to me'" (Judges 14:2–3).

Remember that we don't have to travel far; the distance is not the issue. Neglecting to pray is the issue. Samson did not follow his parents' example of praying for God's direction. Samson's parents prayed to get all the information they needed to raise Samson to fulfill his role—to deliver Israel from the Philistines. This is why Samson was in Timnah, which belonged to Samson's family, but the Philistines had taken control of the area. Samson was there to pick a fight with the Philistines.

As we will see, Samson knew about his unusual strength and his calling, but he aimlessly wandered into self-gratifying pursuits. Going to Timnah and lusting after the beautiful Philistine women was not the optimal way to deliver Israel from Philistine oppression. Samson needed to confront the Philistines, but without prayer, the beautiful women of Timnah distracted him. He did not pray to God about attacking the Philistines, and the lust in his eyes led him off his mission. He was strong and could fight, and God still used him, but Samson did not function at the top of his game. He underused the power entrusted to him.

This is what happens to numerous top athletes today. They fall in love, and they lose their edge. Falling in love is not the real problem; it's what the young athlete does when she falls in love. Instead of praying about properly managing the relationship, the young athlete pursues self-gratification. She spends more and more time with her boyfriend, enjoying sexual relations and pleasing him, and going out with him and having fun together. The young athlete then stops doing their extra training to keep her edge, shows up late to practice and is tired, distracted, and unprepared. As she falls deeper into lust and enjoying sexual relations and sleeping with her boyfriend, she can no longer compete at the highest level. The young athlete loses her spot, her scholarships, and the opportunity to play professionally, and she ends up spending her life talking about how good she used to be and how she wishes she had another opportunity to properly focus on the game.

This is what happened in Samson's world. Samson demanded that one of his enemy's women be his wife. Samson said, "I saw a woman in Timnah, one of the daughters of the Philistines; now therefore, get her for me as a wife" (Judges 14:2).

Samson's mission was not to go down and lust after and marry one of the enemy's women. Samson's parents tried to warn him about marrying someone from an uncircumcised nation. The Philistines were one of the groups that Israel was supposed to destroy, but instead, Israel started worshiping their idol gods along with the idol gods of other ungodly nations.

Marrying a Philistine woman was bad news; it was against his parents' teaching and against the Word of God—and the Philistines were the enemy.

God had issues with an uncircumcised Israelite; therefore, Samson marrying into an uncircumcised nation was a serious problem for God.

"This is My covenant, which you shall keep, between Me and you and your descendants after you: every male among you shall be circumcised. And you shall be circumcised in the flesh of your foreskin, and it shall be the sign of the covenant between Me and you" (Genesis 17:10–11).

"But an uncircumcised male who is not circumcised in the flesh of his foreskin, that person shall be cut off from his people; he has broken My covenant" (Genesis 17:14).

What was driving Samson? He wasn't praying to God or acting on clear direction from God. The lust of Samson's eyes dominated his decision-making. Look at what Samson said after his parents warned him to leave that woman alone: "Get her for me, for she looks good to me" (Judges 14:3).

Something about those beautiful Philistine women messed up Samson's focus on his true mission; they messed up the boy's mind.

Unfortunately, this happens far too often to us in the body of Christ. We pastors and other leaders in the body lose focus on doing God's will because our decision-making is dominated by the lust of our eyes.

Do not get lost in the human element. Do not focus on leaders who are stuck on the lust of their eyes. Realize that despite who or what is off track and going wrong, God is still in control.

"However, his father and mother did not know that it was of the LORD, for He was seeking an occasion against the Philistines. Now at that time the Philistines were ruling over Israel" (Judges 14:4).

God planned to use Samson's action as an opportunity to deal with the Philistines. Yes, Samson was lusting after the enemy's women and neglected to pray like his parents. Yes, Samson could have been much more effective if he would have obeyed his parents and stayed close to God, but God was still in control.

Despite the human element, God permits certain things to happen because despite what humans do or do not do. God has an overriding plan to accomplish His purpose to restore humans back to Him. God is still in control, and His desire will be done on earth, just as it is in heaven.

Where in your life are you wandering into self-gratifying pursuits?

The simply way to check is look at your prayer life. Have you talked to God and sought His face regarding His plan for your life?

Are you genuinely acknowledging God in all your ways so that God will direct you or keep your paths straight? (Proverbs 3:5–6).

What can you do to stop aimlessly wandering into self-gratifying pursuits? The simple answer is to stop to pray. The hard part, though, is stopping. The human habit of leaning on our own understanding instead of stopping to acknowledge God in all our ways is easy to say but difficult to practice.

The best way to fight this struggle is simply to slow down and stop to pray. Be intentional about acknowledging God's presence and power throughout the day, and talk to Him about things. You know how some people talk to themselves all day? Do a similar thing but instead of chatting to yourself, engage God. Recognize that God has the plan, not you. Acknowledge that God knows what is best not you. Recognize who God really is, and humbly ask Him for guidance. Stop and pray! Because you are God's servant, and I am God's servant, what happens to us when God's servants neglect to pray? We easily compromise our godly values.

Samson did not stop to pray, and he struggled with what was right or wrong. He seemed to act based on his feelings—external beauty (14:7) and anger (14:19). Pay attention, and do not get lost in how Samson was out of control. Don't get lost in how easy it is for us to do just like Samson and compromise our godly values.

Samson followed through on meeting the woman he wanted to marry. With all the warning signs, Samson was not moved one bit. He continued his pursuit to marry one of the enemy's women. "Then Samson went down to Timnah with his father and mother, and came as far as the vineyards of Timnah; and behold, a young lion came roaring toward him" (Judges 14:5).

Lions did exist in the land of Israel back then, but why did this lion come after Samson? We are not sure, but we do know that God protected Samson from death at that point.

"Then Samson went down to Timnah with his father and mother, and came as far as the vineyards of Timnah; and behold, a young lion came roaring toward him. The Spirit of the LORD came upon him mightily, so that he tore him as one tears a young goat though he had nothing in his hand; but he did not tell his father or mother what he had done" (Judges 14:5–6).

Samson was sure of his unusual power and knew how to use that power. Since Samson destroyed a young lion, surely the Philistines were no match for Samson.

Samson had no fear of the Philistines because he knew God was with him, and God was going to use him to cause great damage to the Philistines and deliver Israel from them. The teachings of Samson's parents were in his heart.

Here's one last question to ponder: When we neglect to pray, why are we so willing to drag innocent people into our sinful behavior? Spiritual misery loves company. Keeping close and having ongoing company with spiritually miserable people will hurt your spiritual growth, even when you are trying to do right (1 Corinthians 15:33).

Samson had his mother and father in Timnah, while he was pursuing self-gratification and violating his spiritual values. This is what happens when we neglect to pray. We drag innocent people, even the people who love us, into our stuff, even our dangerous stuff.

After the lion attack, Samson continued his pursuit of one of the enemy's women. "So he went down and talked to the woman; and she looked good to Samson" (Judges 14:7).

We continue to see Samson's physical attraction toward this Philistine woman. He could not get his mind off her physical beauty. Notice that any expression of Samson's heartfelt love for the woman is missing.

When locked in on satisfying our personal desires, our self-gratification will lead us to violate our values. We will ignore the

Word of God, we will ignore the conviction of the Holy Spirit in our hearts, and we will step into our wrongdoing as if we are right.

Samson did not think twice about violating his Nazirite vow (Numbers 6:6–8). "When he returned later to take her, he turned aside to look at the carcass of the lion; and behold, a swarm of bees and honey were in the body of the lion (Judges 14:8).

As a Nazirite, should Samson have exposed himself to dead bodies?

> Again the Lord spoke to Moses, saying, "Speak to the sons of Israel and say to them, 'When a man or woman makes a special vow, the vow of a Nazirite, to dedicate himself to the Lord... All the days of his separation to the Lord he shall not go near to a dead person. He shall not make himself unclean for his father or for his mother, for his brother or for his sister, when they die, because his separation to God is on his head. All the days of his separation he is holy to the Lord.'" (Numbers 6:1–2, 6–8).

Samson turned and walked over to the dead body of the lion and even touched it. He did not think twice about being around the dead lion.

Going after that woman seemed to desensitize Samson. He did not seem to feel bad about disobeying God's Word. Perhaps he thought, *Honey in a dead body? Let me get some!*

This is how some of us operate. We see little Jo Jo smoking weed, and we do not think or pray; we just rush in. *Man! Let me hit that!* Without prayer, desensitization to the Word of God becomes our norm.

This desensitization goes deeper. "So he scraped the honey into his hands and went on, eating as he went. When he came to his father and mother, he gave some to them and they ate it; but he did not tell them that he had scraped the honey out of the body of the lion (Judges 14:9).

Samson withheld information from his parents regarding how he violated God's Word to give honey to them. Withholding such information was a form of dishonesty and deception.

Why tell them? He might have thought. *They are just going to confront me with what is right. What they don't know won't hurt them. They are going to follow God's Word, and I don't want my parents holding me accountable right now. I'll just not tell them.*

How many of us are withholding information from the people who love us because we do not want them to hold us accountable? We simply don't want to hear what is right.

> Then his father went down to the woman; and Samson made a feast there, for the young men customarily did this. When they saw him, they brought thirty companions to be with him. Then Samson said to them, "Let me now propound a riddle to you; if you will indeed tell it to me within the seven days of the feast, and find it out, then I will give you thirty linen wraps and thirty changes of clothes. "But if you are unable to tell me, then you shall give me thirty linen wraps and thirty changes of clothes." And they said to him, "Propound your riddle, that we may hear it." So he said to them, "Out of the eater came something to eat, And out of the strong came something sweet." But they could not tell the riddle in three days. Then it came about on the fourth day that they said to Samson's

wife, "Entice your husband, so that he will tell us the riddle, or we will burn you and your father's house with fire. Have you invited us to impoverish us? Is this not so?" Samson's wife wept before him and said, "You only hate me, and you do not love me; you have propounded a riddle to the sons of my people, and have not told it to me." And he said to her, "Behold, I have not told it to my father or mother; so should I tell you?" However she wept before him seven days while their feast lasted. And on the seventh day he told her because she pressed him so hard. She then told the riddle to the sons of her people. (Judges 14:10–17)

As Samson "played with fire," the woman he demanded as his wife betrayed him.

Judges 14 is not about Samson's outsmarting the thirty young Philistine men who came to his wedding party by traveling twenty-three miles away and killing thirty Philistines to pay the young men thirty linen wraps and thirty changes of clothing. The end of Judges 14 is about how Samson played with fire and "got burned."

The enemy's woman, whom Samson hotly pursued because he loved the way she looked physically, betrayed him. After all, she was one of the enemy's women.

The woman did the cry-and-beg routine and played as if she and Samson were supposed to have no secrets between them. What was she really up to? Look at Judges 14:17 again: "However she wept before him seven days while their feast lasted. And on the seventh day he told her because she pressed him so hard. She then told the riddle to the sons of her people."

You can be God's servant and still get off track and start playing with fire—a little bit here and a little bit there, getting by here and getting by over there, withholding information from the people who love you, sneaking around, and slipping and sliding and dipping and dodging. Oh yes, you can come to church and feel the power of God. Yes, God is with you. Yes, you really felt the power of God, and it was real, but if you keep playing with fire, you get burned.

You might get by today, but you will not get away tomorrow.

You might withhold information from the people who love you because you do not want to hear truth, but the rightness they tell you out of love will come back to confront you.

After all the drama, Samson never got the woman (verse 20). The betrayal was not the end of Samson's problems here. Something else happened at the very end of Judges 14. The woman for whom Samson lusted, the woman for whom Samson disregarded his parents, the woman for whom Samson came under attack by a lion, the woman for whom Samson disobeyed the Word of God, the woman to whom Samson told his secret for, the beautiful woman for whom Samson compromised his values—that woman ended up with another man.

> So the men of the city said to him on the seventh day before the sun went down, "What is sweeter than honey? And what is stronger than a lion?" And he said to them, "If you had not plowed with my heifer, You would not have found out my riddle." Then the Spirit of the Lord came upon him mightily, and he went down to Ashkelon and killed thirty of them and took their spoil and gave the changes of clothes to those who told the riddle. And his anger burned, and he went up to his father's house But Samson's wife was given to his companion who had been his friend. (Judges 14:18–20)

We need to learn a lesson from Samson. We need to see what happens when God's servants neglect to pray. We aimlessly wander into self-gratifying pursuits, and we easily compromise our godly values.

We must ask this question: is all the drama involved in ignoring God's plan for our lives worth it?

Here is a prayer to help:

Dear Lord, I want to draw close to you and stay close to you through my prayer life. Lord, help me to talk to you so that I am not stuck, aimlessly wandering into self-gratifying pursuits, and so that I do not ignore my Christian values. Lord, I never want to hurt anyone's spiritual growth by my actions. Please help me to experience the power of the Holy Spirit inside of me, keeping me in an attitude of prayer throughout the day. Lord, thank You for never being too busy and always inclining your ear to hear my prayers. Lord, I love you deeply, and I will call on you all the days of my life. Amen.

CHAPTER 9

Defeating the Spirit of Revenge

Judges 15; Romans 12:17–21; 13:1–7; Matthew 5:44; 6:12–15

Our society is preoccupied with inflicting injury on others for what they did to us. YouTube has an extensive library of all sorts of revenge videos—from car destruction, to violent encounters. You can look at the titles and recognize stuff that you just cannot watch because it is out of control. Posting nude pictures of your ex-wife or ex-husband or boyfriend or girlfriend without that person's permission is evil and cruel, and our national legislators made revenge pornography illegal. Revenge pornography is a crime in the United Kingdom and in the United States.

The spirit of revenge is real. Can you remember a time when someone did something hurtful to you, and you returned the hurt?

The spirit of revenge can take over your life. You might find yourself enraged and breaking a window, hitting someone, posting a damaging video on the Internet, or losing your temper while driving. You even might find yourself picking up a gun and shooting someone in a crime of passion. People can hurt you so deeply and make you so angry!

The spirit of revenge can lead us to do things that we eventually regret.

Perhaps you are seeking revenge for something that someone did to you. Your heart is heavy, you are hurting, you are angry, and you cannot wait to hurt the person who hurt you. My prayer is that, if the spirit of revenge is on you today, after you read this chapter, you will submit your heart to God and allow Him to help you to forgive so you can experience freedom.

How do we defeat the spirit of revenge? Revenge, like anything else that damages human relationships, can be and must be defeated.

The answer to this question is in a lesson from a biblical character who spent his life seeking revenge. Then we will look at some specific biblical action steps to defeat revenge.

Recognize That Revenge Reduces Our
Effectiveness (Judges 15:1-20).

How do we defeat the spirit of revenge? Recognize that revenge reduces our effectiveness. The story of Samson is a powerful lesson. God appeared to Samson's parents and informed them that their son would be a superhero. Samson was dedicated to God at birth because God picked him to deliver Israel from Philistine oppression.

We've seen how Samson neglected to pray for God's direction as his parents did, and Samson aimlessly wandered into self-gratifying pursuits. He traveled four to six miles from home down to Timnah to pick a fight with the Philistines, and he lost his mind over the physical beauty of one of the Philistine women. When he told his parents to get her for him as a wife, Samson's parents tried to warn him, but Samson insisted on having one of the enemy's women. "Get her for me, for she looks good to me" (Judges 14:3).

Samson, ignored his parents and went to Timnah, messing around with the enemy, and married one of the enemy's women. He then learned a painfully burning lesson.

Judges 14 ends with sad consequences for Samson's messing around with the wrong woman. The woman's father gave her to another man (Judges 14:20, cf. 15:2).

Judges 15 opens with interesting news. "But after a while, in the time of wheat harvest, Samson visited his wife with a young goat, and said, 'I will go in to my wife in her room.' But her father did not let him enter" (Judges 15:1).

In Judges 15, we see that while on the wrong mission, Samson sought revenge over the wrong woman.

Remember that Samson was called to deliver Israel, not to visit their female enemies. How are you similar to Samson? Perhaps you are doing something unrelated to your calling, and you are off course.

The wife—the woman that Samson went to visit—is the same woman who betrayed him. In Judges 14, Samson's wife cried and begged him to tell her the answer to the riddle he proposed to the Philistine men at their wedding party. The wife got the answer from Samson and gave the answer to the Philistines. Samson had to pay because his wife betrayed him.

The father of Samson's wife then gave her to another man. At that point, Samson could have opened his eyes and realized that God saved his neck from being involved with the wrong women. Instead of refocusing on his mission, however, Samson sought revenge.

> Her father said, "I really thought that you hated her
> intensely; so I gave her to your companion. Is not her
> younger sister more beautiful than she? Please let her
> be yours instead." Samson then said to them, "This
> time I shall be blameless in regard to the Philistines
> when I do them harm." Samson went and caught
> three hundred foxes, and took torches, and turned
> the foxes tail to tail and put one torch in the middle

between two tails. When he had set fire to the torches, he released the foxes into the standing grain of the Philistines, thus burning up both the shocks and the standing grain, along with the vineyards and groves. (Judges 15:2–5)

What was Samson's reaction? Was it prayer to God? No! The spirit of revenge was on Samson. "This time I shall be blameless in regard to the Philistines when I do them harm." I will destroy the Philistines food supply.

Samson was not supposed to have a peace accord with the Philistines! God called Samson to deliver Israel from the Philistines' stronghold.

After his revenge, Samson still did not get the woman (verse 6).

"While messing around with the wrong woman, and doing his revenge thing, Samson destroyed the Philistines' food supply. Look at what happened next: "Then the Philistines said, 'Who did this?' And they said, 'Samson, the son-in-law of the Timnite, because he took his wife and gave her to his companion.' So the Philistines came up and burned her and her father with fire" (Judges 15:6).

Therefore, the Philistines got revenge against Samson.

All the stuff Samson went through to get the wrong woman was in vain. He disregarded his parent's advice. He disobeyed the Word of God. He got attacked by a young lion. He violated his Nazirite vow by touching a dead lion's body. He was betrayed by his wife. He killed thirty men to pay off his debt because of his wife's betrayal. Then he left his wife and went home to his daddy's house, angry (Judges 14:3–20).

Samson cooled off and came back to be with his wife, but she no longer was his wife. Samson never had the opportunity to visit the woman who was supposed to be his wife. The Philistines killed her because of his revenge upon them.

Samson was in a big mess! Look at Samson's next action, motivated by revenge. Samson said to them, "Since you act like this, I will surely take revenge on you, but after that I will quit" (Judges 15:7).

Samson used the "R" word. In the Bible, God is the one who is to take revenge on people for their evil, and God is the one who gives humans instructions on how to handle the evil of others. Humans are to act under God's direction, not take matters into their own hands.

Samson said, "I will surely take revenge on you, but after that I will quit." He would hurt them because they killed his wife, but after taking revenge, he would stop. (Look at Judges 15:2–5.) Did God call Samson to quit? God called Samson to deliver Israel from the Philistines. God wanted to use Samson to deal with the Philistines, but Samson adopted a personal revenge-based agenda. Despite Samson's motives, God worked His plan (verse 8; cf. 14:4, 13:5).

What in the world was God doing while Samson was off his mission, seeking revenge? "He struck them ruthlessly with a great slaughter; and he went down and lived in the cleft of the rock of Etam" (Judges 15:8).

Despite Samson's motives, God worked His plan. God's plan was to use Samson to deliver Israel from the Philistines. Yes, Samson was off track, but God still used some of the off-track stuff that Samson did to break the Philistines' stronghold on Israel.

Don't get too excited here, thinking you can get off track, and somehow God will bless your off-track behavior. Look at how Samson's off-track actions endangered his fellow Israelites: "Then the Philistines went up and camped in Judah, and spread out in Lehi. The men of Judah said, 'Why have you come up against us?' And they said, 'We have come up to bind Samson in order to do to him as he did to us'" (Judges 15:9–10).

Our actions affect other people. Because of Samson's actions, the Philistines, who already oppressed Israel, camped in Judah, to capture

Samson. Innocent people could have gotten hurt in the Philistines' efforts to capture Samson.

People aimlessly wandering into self-gratifying pursuits do not think about how they hurt, inconvenience, or endanger the people around them; they are too stuck on themselves.

You must not focus so intensely on getting revenge that you put innocent lives in danger.

How many times are there innocent victims of drive-by shootings because someone was seeking revenge? This could have happened to Samson's fellow Israelites when the Philistines were trying to get revenge on Samson for his revenge on them.

Here is another twist on how revenge reduces our effectiveness:

> Then 3,000 men of Judah went down to the cleft of the rock of Etam and said to Samson, "Do you not know that the Philistines are rulers over us? What then is this that you have done to us?" And he said to them, "As they did to me, so I have done to them." They said to him, "We have come down to bind you so that we may give you into the hands of the Philistines." And Samson said to them, "Swear to me that you will not kill me." So they said to him, "No, but we will bind you fast and give you into their hands; yet surely we will not kill you." Then they bound him with two new ropes and brought him up from the rock. (Judges 15:11–13)

What did Samson really have here? He had access to three thousand men of Judah. Samson was the designated deliverer of Israel. All he had to do was rally these men of Israel for war. Samson had God's favor, so God would have brought Israel's army together for Samson, just as He did for Gideon. If Samson killed one thousand Philistines by himself, think about the great victory they could have had together.

What was the problem? Samson was stuck on personal revenge. Despite Samson's motives, God still worked His plan. Let's look:

> When he came to Lehi, the Philistines shouted as they met him. And the Spirit of the LORD came upon him mightily so that the ropes that were on his arms were as flax that is burned with fire, and his bonds dropped from his hands. He found a fresh jawbone of a donkey, so he reached out and took it and killed a thousand men with it. Then Samson said, "With the jawbone of a donkey, Heaps upon heaps, With the jawbone of a donkey I have killed a thousand men." When he had finished speaking, he threw the jawbone from his hand; and he named that place Ramath-lehi. (Judges 15:14–17)

This is the famous scene where Samson killed one thousand Philistines with the jawbone of a donkey. Samson's motives were off the mission, but God still worked His overriding plan to break the stronghold the Philistines had on Israel. God was in control, despite Samson's personal revenge.

Can you imagine what Samson's godly parents were thinking about their son by his going after the enemy's women and putting the nation's safety in jeopardy? *Lord, where did we go wrong? Lord, what is going to happen with our son? Lord, why is not our son doing what you called him to do?*

Despite what our children are doing or not doing, God is still in control. God's plan is much bigger than our children's plans. God's plan is not dependent on our children, and God will accomplish His plan, with or without our children.

Keep praying for your children, and keep your eyes on God. As we see in the case of Samson, God still worked His plan; in our case, God will still work His plan with the children entrusted to our care.

At the end of Judges 15, we finally get to hear Samson pray. This is the first of Samson's two recorded prayers. What kind of prayer did Samson pray?

> Then he became very thirsty, and he called to the Lord and said, "You have given this great deliverance by the hand of Your servant, and now shall I die of thirst and fall into the hands of the uncircumcised?" But God split the hollow place that is in Lehi so that water came out of it. When he drank, his strength returned and he revived. Therefore he named it En-hakkore, which is in Lehi to this day. So he judged Israel twenty years in the days of the Philistines. (Judges 15:18–20)

Samson prayed a post-revenge, self-preservation prayer. It was as if he said, "Lord, I know that after all the power you gave me to beat these Philistines, You won't let me die of thirst and fall into their hands." Samson, however, did not thank God for saving his life and giving him such a huge victory. Killing one thousand soldiers with the jawbone of a donkey gives us a picture of how strong and powerful God made Samson. Why couldn't Samson simply stop and praise the Lord?

Why was Samson doing all his fighting alone? Each of Samson's four recorded fights in the book of Judges were because of what someone did to him. Everything was personal with Samson. With his supernatural strength from the Lord and with the calling of God on his life, Samson worked alone and limited his success. In twenty years of judging Israel, Samson's episodes of revenge limited his effectiveness to killing approximate six thousand Philistines. Samson teaches us that when driven by revenge, we reduce our effectiveness.

Is the spirit of revenge driving your activities?

- Samson's success was limited because he allowed personal revenge to drive him. Is your success limited because you are allowing personal revenge to drive you?
- Should you be angry and seek revenge, or should you seek God's will for your response to the evil and hurt that people do to you?

How do we defeat the spirit of revenge? We defeat the spirit of revenge with biblical actions (Romans 12:17–21; 13:1–6; Matthew 5:44; 6:12–15).

Seeking God's will for our response will help us defeat the spirit of revenge. Let's review what God says about revenge.

> Never pay back evil for evil to anyone. Respect what is right in the sight of all men. If possible, so far as it depends on you, be at peace with all men. Never take your own revenge, beloved, but leave room for the wrath *of God*, for it is written, "VENGEANCE IS MINE, I WILL REPAY," says the Lord. "BUT IF YOUR ENEMY IS HUNGRY, FEED HIM, AND IF HE IS THIRSTY, GIVE HIM A DRINK; FOR IN SO DOING YOU WILL HEAP BURNING COALS ON HIS HEAD." Do not be overcome by evil, but overcome evil with good. (Romans 12:17–21)

What God says about revenge is not the norm in our society. People are not trying to overcome evil with good. People are not trying to be nice to the people who hurt them. People are not trying to get out of the way and leave room for God's wrath to come upon people who hurt them. People are not trying to make peace with the people who hurt them. The norm in our society is that people return evil for evil. The Internet is full of real-life cases of people getting revenge. In fact, the Internet is the first place many people go to seek answers to their life challenges. When they Google their issues, sometimes hundreds of responses appear.

The sad reality is that Christians also get caught up in the Google search versus the God search.

Instead of looking for what our Google search says, we need to look for what our God search says. God says to do the opposite of the social norm. God says to overcome evil with good!

Let the proper authorities handle wrongful and criminal actions against you. God gives us a proper process with which to handle wrongful and criminal actions against us. God gives the responses for the individual, the church, and the government.

If someone does a wrongful, noncriminal action against you that hurts you, you have a biblical role. "If your brother sins, go and show him his fault in private; if he listens to you, you have won your brother. But if he does not listen *to you*, take one or two more with you, so that BY THE MOUTH OF TWO OR THREE WITNESSES EVERY FACT MAY BE CONFIRMED (Matthew 18:15–16).

God says that your first action is to confront the person who hurt you. This doesn't refer to confronting a rapist, or carjacker, or person who is physically hurting you (get the police to help in violent cases). This refers to a nonviolent wrongful action against you. Your first action is to confront the person with the wrongful action against you, such as:

- You broke your promise.
- You hurt my feelings.
- You did something inappropriate with my spouse.
- What you posted on the Internet about me was wrong.
- What you said was hurtful.
- The way you treat me makes me feel undervalued and unappreciated.
- Your tone of voice is offensive.

When you confront the person, you are to speak truth in love (Ephesians 4:15). Jesus says that if the person listens to you, you have won him or her. You have the basis for reconciliation.

What if the person is a believer but refuses to listen? This is when the church has a specific role in the conflict. "If he refuses to listen to them, tell it to the church; and if he refuses to listen even to the church, let him be to you as a Gentile and a tax collector" (Matthew 18:17).

If the person cooperates with the spiritual leaders in the church, then the church leaders can put a plan for reconciliation in place and follow through with the parties involved.

If the person refuses to cooperate with the church leadership, Jesus said that then the church leaders are to put the person on church discipline (let him be to you as a Gentile and tax collector). This is not a pretty picture; it gives the picture of serious discipline.

In 2 Thessalonians, God gives us some insight on how the church deals practically with a person as a Gentile and a tax collector. Look at it: "If anyone does not obey our instruction in this letter, take special note of that person and do not associate with him, so that he will be put to shame. Yet do not regard him as an enemy, but admonish him as a brother" (2 Thessalonians 3:14–15).

We must confront the person and even prevent the person from doing ministry. He or she must be under constant supervision, and we must get the person in specialized programs. We must get him or her professional counseling, do one-on-one intensive discipleship or counseling, turn him or her into the authorities, and, as a last resort, remove the person from the fellowship. In all of our actions, we must still love the person because he or she is a fellow Christian. We do not allow the person's sinful behavior to continue in the church or toward a fellow Christian or non-Christian outside of the church.

The church loves people back to health.

The next level of action to overcome the spirit of revenge is to report a person's criminal action or the wrongful action to governmental authorities.

For instance, if a person raped someone, physically abused someone, or is stalking, cyber-bullying, or posing a threat to someone, we are to go to the local police and get help. Pastors or other leaders should lead this process. The police will come to the church and help out, but we must call them for help.

Romans 13:1–6 describes the role of government in maintaining order in society.

The key piece, on our part, is to make sure we do not call the police or other authorities for false claims. We cannot lie about other people and put them in the criminal justice system falsely.

Teach children that if they are verbally, physically, or sexually abused they must tell their parents so they can help the children.

If the abuser is a parent, relative, or a person in authority, such as a church worker, teacher, and so on, the child must call the police, a counselor, an aunt or uncle, their pastor, or someone they trust who will listen to them and get help.

Teach children that they must not make false claims against someone because they are mad at a parent, for example, for not letting them have their way.

Parents should remember that it's not against to law to take away your child's access to the car or his or her cell phone. It's not against the law to monitor what is on your child's cell phone or computer. It's not against the law the take your children's bedroom door off the hinges if they continue locking themselves in and disobeying you.

You have authority, as the parent, to discipline your child and fight for his or her well-being. Stop allowing a child's threats to disempower you. State the consequences for your child's behavior, and stick with them. Keep it simple: "If you do right, you receive blessings. If you do wrong, you receive consequences."

In regard to physical spankings, I recommend that parents speak with local police leaders. In some cities, police will support parents who properly administer a few swats to the backsides of disobedient children (Proverbs 13:24). Police can and will give you the proper guidelines, if spanking is permitted in your city. In many cities, it is legal to spank our children, but it is illegal to abuse them. I mention the police because when we refuse to discipline our children, and children think no one is going to challenge their negative behavior, they usually get worse, and the police have to pick them up for violence toward teachers and others in authority or peers and for breaking the law. Police know that when parents do not hold children accountable for inappropriate behavior, the children assume that nothing will happen to them. Before we know it, we have another citizen who feels he or she does not have to listen to people in authority and who functions as if he or she is above the law.

They will become comfortable stealing, driving drunk, cursing their parents, disrespecting their teachers and then employers and customers, and ignoring people in authority. Eventually, the police will have to get involved in that (eventually grown-up) child's life to enforce the laws he or she has no problem breaking.

Here is another biblical action to help destroy the spirit of revenge: love, forgive, and pray for the person who mistreated you. In Matthew 5:44, Jesus said, "But I say to you, love your enemies and pray for those who persecute you."

The word *persecute* means to organize a program to oppress and harass people.[10] When people intentionally put you down and harass you, or when people intentionally do things to hurt you or people around you, Jesus gave two non-negotiable commands: love them and pray for them.

We are to show care and concern for the people who constantly do things to hurt us, and we are to talk to God about those people. For example, we might say, "God, please help me to love them, and please stop them from doing evil. God, please change their hearts. God, please save their souls. God, please heal our relationship. God, please do something to get their attention, and get them to stop." We need to talk to God about "bad people" instead of taking matters into our own hands.

In Matthew 6:12, Jesus commanded us to include forgiveness in our prayers: "And forgive us our debts, as we also have forgiven our debtors."

Jesus also said, "For if you forgive others for their transgressions, your heavenly Father will also forgive you. But if you do not forgive others, then your Father will not forgive your transgressions" (Matthew 6:14–15).

We must forgive people for the wrong they did to us. We must release people—let them go and stop holding their wrongdoing toward us against them. Release them, and let them go.

---

[10] Johannes P. Louw and Eugene Albert Nida, *Greek-English Lexicon of the New Testament: Based on Semantic Domains* (New York: United Bible Societies, 1996), 498.

We give people too much power over us when we constantly think about and cry about what they did to us. When you hurt innocent people because of what someone else did to you, the person who actually hurt you has too much power over you. You cannot allow another human to control your emotions, your reactions, and your decisions. Forgive! Release them, and let them go!

Love, prayer, and forgiveness kill the spirit of revenge.

Deal with the spirit of revenge. First, recognize that the spirit of revenge will reduce your effectiveness. When you preoccupy yourself with revenge, you will lose sight of God's call on your life and will become a slave to inflicting hurt on the person who hurt you. You must not give people that kind of power over you.

In order to break free from someone's power over you and destroy the spirit of revenge, take biblical actions. Review what God says about revenge. Stop being a victim, and take the steps to properly deal with the people who hurt you.

Here is a personal prayer to help:

Lord, thank you for this lesson from the life of Samson. Lord, search my heart and see if I am pursuing something with the wrong motives. Lord, see if I am wrongly using your resources to inflict injury on someone because of what that person did. Lord, I do not want impure motives to hinder your call on my life. Father, destroy the spirit of revenge in my heart. Give me wisdom regarding how to respond to mistreatment, and help me to love, pray, and forgive. Father, with the time and resources you grant me, maximize my efforts to bring peace and biblical values to my family, my community, my work, my school, my church, and beyond. Use me for your glory. In Jesus's name, I pray. Amen.

CHAPTER 10

God's Windows of Opportunities

Judges 16

God gives His children windows of opportunity that connect to fulfilling His call on our lives. God's windows of opportunity consists of our doing good works. In Ephesians, the Bible says, "For we are His workmanship, created in Christ Jesus for good works, which God prepared beforehand so that we would walk in them" (Ephesians 2:10).

God calls us to work for Him and gives us opportunities to work for Him. When people see our good works—and they will—and we deflect attention off ourselves and onto God, we demonstrate the essence of bringing glory to God.

Jesus said, "Let your light shine before men in such a way that they may see your good works, and glorify your Father who is in heaven" (Matthew 5:16).

God is not interested in sharing the stage in the universe with us as if we are equals. God will bless us, and we will share in His glory, but we are not equals with God. Hence, we do not make the agenda. We do not determine what we will do for God. We do not renegotiate our assignment from God. We do not delegate our assignment from God to someone else.

God will show us the open windows of ministry opportunity, and we are to step out with His power and serve Him.

If God gave you the spiritual gift of teaching, you can start a prayer group in your home and have a short Bible lesson. You can send out YouTube Bible study lessons. You can lead a Bible study at school, work, home, church, and so on.

An evangelist has an unusual burden to reach the lost for Christ. Witness at the grocery store, the gym, a restaurant, and to your neighbors. Instead of hanging up on the telemarketers, witness to them. Instead of being rude to the customer service representatives from foreign countries, witness overseas from home. Ask them what they know about Jesus. Boldly share the message of Jesus with them. Before you hang up, compliment them on their English, and thank them for their help. Even if you do not like it, businesses operate in a global economy today. Make the ministry adjustment, and see your contact with people from other countries as a window of opportunity to witness for Jesus.

Ask your server at a restaurant if you can pray for him or her about something. Then pray a short prayer. Give the server a witnessing tract, or write the church name, address, and website on a napkin for your server, and invite him or her to church. Show love and respect and thank him or her for the service. As our older generation would say, "You get more bees with honey than with vinegar."

With your gift of helps, volunteer to visit a sick person and read scripture and pray with the person. Text message words of encouragement to someone you have not seen at church, and follow up with a call and/or a visit. Volunteer to help someone move to a new location. Clean up, or help someone learn how to use his or her cell phone. Open the car door, help with the groceries, cut someone's lawn or wash his or her car, and so forth. *Stop watching windows of opportunity close day after day.*

Too many Christians have a frozen-ministry mentality because of the distractions of everyday life, and they watch the windows of ministry opportunity close every day.

Let's look at God's windows of opportunity from the life of Samson.

When we're distracted, numerous windows close, and we become numb and stop caring. Far too many believers are numb and on the sidelines. The church of Christ is missing out on huge victories for Christ. The primary reason for our closed ministry windows is that we're distracted. We are doing everything else but sharing the message of Jesus and building people up in the faith.

Let's look at Samson's life, and gain some insight into God's windows of opportunity.

The first such insight from Samson's life is that God closes main windows of opportunity when we are too distracted. What led to Samson's main windows (big opportunities) closing?

We know that God chose and empowered Samson to deliver Israel from the Philistines. Samson displayed superhuman strength in several instances—he killed a lion with his hands, he killed thirty Philistines in one setting, he struck the Philistines ruthlessly with a great slaughter, and he killed one thousand Philistines with the jawbone of a donkey.

Although Samson was preoccupied with getting revenge on the Philistines, and his success was limited, God gave Samson power and success every time he went to battle.

God, however, eventually closed Samson's main window—his big opportunity to have huge victories over the Philistines during his twenty years as a Judge over Israel.

What led to the end of Samson's opportunities for these huge victories? He dismissed his parent's advice (Judges 14:3).

Samson went four to six miles from his home to Timnah and saw a beautiful Philistine woman, and he asked his parents to get her for him. Samson's parents advised him against getting with the enemy's women. All of Samson's women were Philistine women, and his parents never approved of any of them.

Samson also disobeyed God's Word by violating His Nazirite vow. His first violation occurred when he touched the dead body of the lion (Judges 14:8–9; cf. Numbers 6:6–8). Then Samson did not tell his parents that he violated his Nazirite vow when he took honey from the dead lion's body and gave it to them.

We later will see that Samson cut his hair, which also was an act of disobedience to God (Judges 16:19; cf. 13:5; Numbers 6:5).

Why did God close Samson's window of opportunity for numerous huge victories against the Philistines? It was because Samson disregarded dangerous distractions to his calling. Samson's first wife was a dangerous distraction (Judges 14–15). Remember that his first Philistine woman betrayed him, and Samson had to pay the Philistines for her betrayal. The prostitute in Gaza was another dangerous distraction for Samson (Judges 16:1–4).

Samson went down to Gaza, which was one of the five main cities for the Philistines, and got with a prostitute. While Samson was with the prostitute, the Philistines surrounded the place and waited to kill Samson. In this case, Samson decided to pick up the front gate of the city and carry it about thirty-eight miles uphill to the top of the mountain opposite Hebron. I am not sure why Samson simply didn't slaughter the Philistines waiting to kill him.

I do know that Samson, who was supposed to be dedicated to God, was distracted with that Philistine prostitute and lost another opportunity to break the Philistines' stronghold on Israel. Samson's most dangerous distraction was Delilah (Judges 16:4–21), his third Philistine woman. Look at what happened:

"After this it came about that he loved a woman in the valley of Sorek, whose name was Delilah. The lords of the Philistines came up to her and said to her, 'Entice him, and see where his great strength lies and how we may overpower him that we may bind him to afflict him. Then we will each give you eleven hundred pieces of silver.' So Delilah said to Samson, 'Please tell me where your great strength is and how you may be bound to afflict you'" (Judges 16:4–6).

Samson fell in love with this Philistine woman named Delilah. After Samson had been with Delilah, the scripture tells us that the Philistines got with her and negotiated a lucrative deal to find the secret to his strength so they could overpower him, bind him, and afflict him. The Philistines put a countrywide hit out on Samson—Gaza is along the Mediterranean Coast, about thirty-five miles from Samson's hometown in Zora. The Philistines were out to destroy Samson, and they obviously knew about his weakness for their women.

Samson played a dangerous game with Delilah. She asked him about his source of power; she essentially asked, "How can we imprison you and put you to forced labor? How can we break you down? How can we stop you?"

Samson was betrayed by one Philistine woman, and then he was surrounded by the Philistine army while messing with another Philistine woman. Then Delilah, his third Philistine woman, asked him how she could break him down.

What was wrong with this man? Samson knew that Delilah was up to no good so he played games with her, giving her the answers she wanted:

- Bind me with seven fresh cords that have not been dried. Then I will become weak like other men (Judges 16:7).
- Bind me tightly with new, unused ropes. Then I will become weak like other men (Judges 16:11).

- Weave the seven locks of my hair with the web and fasten it with a pin. Then I will become weak like other men (Judges 16:13).

What happened each time? Delilah brought in the Philistines to break Samson down.

Samson could not connect the pleading for his secret with the pleading and betrayal of his first wife (Judges 16:4–14; cf. 14:12–18).

Delilah had the enemy waiting three times. Why did Samson keep playing games with her? (Judges 16:4–14).

This playing-with-fire business gets really deep when you keep playing.

> Then she said to him, "How can you say, 'I love you,' when your heart is not with me? You have deceived me these three times and have not told me where your great strength is." It came about when she pressed him daily with her words and urged him, that his soul was annoyed to death. So he told her all that was in his heart and said to her, "A razor has never come on my head, for I have been a Nazirite to God from my mother's womb. If I am shaved, then my strength will leave me and I will become weak and be like any other man." (Judges 16:15–17)

Delilah was the enemy's woman. Why did Samson think his secret was safe with her?

Each time that Delilah had the Philistines waiting to break him down, he could have broken them down. He had three excellent opportunities to attack the Philistines, but he wasted each opportunity. Each time his missed his opportunity, he seemed to get weaker and weaker, until Delilah finally got to his heart, and he told her all that was in his heart.

What happened next?

"When Delilah saw that he had told her all that was in his heart, she sent and called the lords of the Philistines, saying, 'Come up once more, for he has told me all that is in his heart.' Then the lords of the Philistines came up to her and brought the money in their hands. She made him sleep on her knees, and called for a man and had him shave off the seven locks of his hair. Then she began to afflict him, and his strength left him" (Judges 16:18–19).

While you are distracted, the enemy knows just when to attack. When distracted by the lust of your flesh and the lust of your eyes, and you think you can dance with the devil, and you open your heart to the devil, then the devil quickly—without hesitation, without guilt, without loyalty, without love—kills, steals, and destroys. The enemy inflicts the greatest pain possible when you least expect it.

Here is the cold part about Samson's situation: while Samson thought he was safe and secure when lying in the devil's lap, the devil "got paid." Delilah got fifty-five hundred pieces of silver, which was approximately 137 pounds of silver. The girl "got paid"! Samson got his haircut, and the woman he trusted began to afflict him—and Samson ended in the fire again. Samson "got burned"!

How did that happen to Samson, the strong man? It happened because Samson disregarded dangerous distractions to his calling. While distracted, Samson's window for huge victories closed. What does this mean? Look again at Judges 16:

"She said, 'The Philistines are upon you, Samson!' And he awoke from his sleep and said, 'I will go out as at other times and shake myself free.' But he did not know that the LORD had departed from him" (Judges 16:20). Samson thought he would pull through, like before.

If you keep playing with fire, you will find out the hard way, just like Samson, that fire burns. Samson played with the Philistines' women repeatedly and thought that he was the man. Samson had a bad case of I-Got-This-itis. He thought he would just get up and handle his business as usual. He thought he would pull through as before. *God's got my back*, he thought. *I know I am wrong to sleep with this Philistine woman who is not my wife, but God understands, and He will pull me through, just like before.*

Because he was distracted, Samson didn't realize that God had closed the main window of opportunity. Look again at the end of verse 20: "But he did not know that the LORD had departed from him."

How did Samson miss the fact that God was not with him in his mess? He took God's power for granted. He was doing his own thing. Samson thought he was getting away with sin in front of God. The old people were right. "You might get by, but you won't get away." God will deal with our sin.

While in sin, you are spiritually weak in your service to God. You go through the motions and play so much in your sin that you do not even know when your true source of power is gone. Everyone else knows you are operating in the flesh, but you don't know. You are so distracted and so out of touch with God that you do not even know how far gone you really are.

You are playing church and offering a dirty heart, a wicked lifestyle, and a bunch of empty service. The devil knows you are playing church. The saints of God know you are playing church. Even the non-Christians can look at you and tell something is wrong. Everybody knows but you. You are too distracted!

Look at what else happened while Samson was distracted.

"Then the Philistines seized him and gouged out his eyes; and they brought him down to Gaza and bound him with bronze chains, and he was a grinder in the prison" (Judges 16:21).

As the scripture tells us, the Philistines captured Samson but did not kill him. They captured Samson, just as they had planned, because they wanted to break him down. They tortured Samson by gouging out his eyes and then by putting Samson to forced labor in prison, where he was made to work hard all day. This was the Philistines plan to break Samson down.

While Samson was distracted, the enemy broke him down. While Samson was distracted, God closed Samson's main window of opportunity to deliver Israel from the Philistines.

Look at Samson's life, and gain insight into God's windows of opportunities. When you are too distracted, God will close your main window of opportunity. God is not going to play games with you. God will give you warnings, but if you continue to ignore God's warnings, He will have to discipline you.

Can you see the specific pattern that led to Samson's getting the main window of opportunity closed in his face? Samson consistently did three things that got him in trouble with God:

- He dismissed his parents' advice.
- He disobeyed God's Word.
- He allowed dangerous distractions to his calling.

Some of us have a similar pattern in our lives. We are off track, and we are in trouble with God.

Here are questions we must ask at this point: how could Samson have gotten back on track? What could have Samson done to avoid God's closing his main window of opportunity?

The real question is, how can we get back to God and get on track?

Just do the opposite of what got you in trouble in the first place. If you are in trouble for speeding, slow down and stop speeding. If you are addicted to alcohol, get help so you can stop drinking. If you are in trouble for sleeping on the job, stay awake and concentrate on your job. If you are in trouble for being a smart-mouth and talking back, stop the negative speech and use positive speech. Say thank you. Say, "How can I help?" Say, "I am sorry. I was wrong. Please forgive me." Say, "How can I do better next time?" Be a source of encouragement.

Doing the opposite of wrong can help you get right,

Samson's Wrongs

- He dismissed his parent's advice.
- He disobeyed God's Word.
- He disregarded dangerous distractions to his calling.

The Opposite of Samson's wrongs

- Wisely draw upon your parents' wisdom.

  My son, do not forget my teaching, But let your heart keep my commandments; For length of days and years of life And peace they will add to you. Do not let kindness and truth leave you; Bind them around your neck, Write them on the tablet of your heart. So you will find favor and good repute In the sight of God and man. Trust in the LORD with all your heart And do not lean on your own understanding. In all your ways acknowledge Him, And He will make your paths straight. (Proverbs 3:1–6)

- Passionately obey God's Word.

  "How can a young man keep his way pure? By keeping it according to Your word. With all my heart I have sought You; Do not let me wander from Your commandments. Your word I have treasured in my heart, That I may not sin against You" (Psalm 119:9–11).

- Pursue God's call on your life to the very end.
  "For I am already being poured out as a drink offering, and the time of my departure has come. I have fought the good fight, I have finished the course, I have kept the faith; in the future there is laid up for me the crown of righteousness, which the Lord, the righteous Judge, will award to me on that day; and not only to me, but also to all who have loved His appearing" (2 Timothy 4:6–8).

What are you doing with the window of opportunity before you today?

Are you so distracted that you do not see your window closing?

Are you so far gone that you do not see that your big window has closed?

God may have closed your main window of opportunity, but I have good news for you. If you get right—if you dare to do the opposite of the wrong you are doing—God has another window for you. God has a mercy window of opportunity for you. (We will talk about God's mercy window in the next chapter.)

Here is a personal prayer to help before you read the final chapter:

Dear Lord, thank you for giving me the story of Samson in the Bible. I see many insights and need your help in applying them to my life. Lord, forgive me for anything I have done to neglect your call on my life. Today, show me afresh your main window or your mercy window of opportunity for me. Father, walk with me so that I trust you instead of leaning on my own understanding. I acknowledge you in everything so that you will direct my path.

Lord, I love you and live to serve you. In the name of Jesus, I pray. Amen.

CHAPTER 11

God's Mercy Window of Opportunities

Judges 16

Samson, the strong man in the Bible, had numerous windows of opportunity to lead huge victories against the Philistines over a period of twenty years, but he was often distracted with seeking revenge over the enemy's women. When Samson messed with Delilah, his third Philistine women, he dropped his guard, and instead of recognizing that he was playing with fire and getting away, Samson continued to play with Delilah.

- Bind me with seven fresh cords that were not dried. Then I will become weak like other men (Judges 16:7).
- Bind me tightly with new, unused ropes. Then I will become weak like other men (Judges 16:11).
- Weave the seven locks of my hair with the web and fasten it with a pin. Then I will become weak like other men (Judges 16:13).

After several days of hanging out with Delilah, Samson was burned by a master player. Delilah pressured Samson into telling her the secret to his strength. Then Delilah had Samson sleep in her lap, and while he was fast asleep, Delilah called in a man to cut Samson's hair.

"She said, 'The Philistines are upon you, Samson!' And he awoke from his sleep and said, 'I will go out as at other times and shake myself free.' But he did not know that the LORD had departed from him" (Judges 16:20).

What a spiritually dark time for Samson. He did not know that the LORD had departed from him. God closed Samson's main window of opportunity

All of the chances for Samson to break the stronghold that the Philistines had on Israel were now gone. Samson could no longer go back to lead Israel's army or destroy the Philistines who laid traps for him. The unexpected irony of Samson's story is that even with God's call on his life and with supernatural strength from God, Samson lost his power and ended up in a Philistine prison.

We expected Samson to do just the opposite of what got him in trouble with God!

We have learned from Samson to look at what we are doing.

This is what Samson did to get into trouble:

- He dismissed his parents' advice.
- He disobeyed God's Word.
- He disregarded dangerous distractions to his calling.

We expected Samson to do the opposite of what got him into trouble with God:

- Wisely draw upon your parents' wisdom (Proverbs 3:1–6).
- Passionately obey God's Word (Psalm 119:9–11).
- Pursue God's call on your life to the very end (2 Timothy 4:6–8).

How are you doing? Are you practicing the opposite of what keeps getting you into trouble? Are you fighting to get things right between you and God and the people you deal with?

God did not give us the story of Samson so that we could have a dramatic story to read. He gave us this story about Samson so that we could learn life lessons.

- If we play with fire, and get too distracted, as Samson did, we will feel the burning fire.
- God is not playing games with us. God will give us some warnings, but if we continue to ignore his warnings, God will close our main window of opportunity.

Samson crossed the line and told Delilah the secret to his strength, and Delilah had his hair cut. Then God closed Samson's main window of opportunity.

We can find a powerful lesson by looking at the end of Samson's life. God has a mercy window of opportunity for his children when we get right with Him.

When God Closes a Main Window, He Still Has a Mercy Window (Judges 16:22–30)

I have some good news for those who got off track in life. I also have good news for those who are still off track today.

Have you already had your Samson experience? Has God just shut the window of opportunity in your face?

Are you playing with God today, and you can sense that you are in trouble with Him and that God is about to close your window of opportunity?

Are you sick and tired of being sick and tired of underachieving and looking at your lost opportunity? Do you want another chance?

Are you are ready for some good news?

When God closes a main window that no one can open, God gets our attention and gives us a chance to get right with Him. When we get right, God opens a mercy window that no one can close.

"However, the hair of his head began to grow again after it was shaved off" (Judges 16:22).

Samson was struggling in prison because he ignored his parents' advice, he kept disobeying God's Word, and he allowed dangerous distractions. Yet while he was humiliated by the Philistines in prison, God's mercy was at work in Samson's life.

The Bible does not say that Samson prayed, "Lord, if you get me out of this one and let my hair grow back, I will serve you." The Bible says that the Philistines seized Samson and gouged out his eyes, they brought him down to Gaza and bound him with bronze chains, and he was a grinder in the prison. Samson was humiliated. The strong man was broken and working in prison.

Just in case you think that your sin and disobedience before God is cute, and your hair is going to automatically grow back without some consequences for your sin, let's take a quick journey to the Philistine Federal Penitentiary at Gaza City.

First, notice that God will send you to prison to stop you in your tracks and to get your attention. Keep playing with fire, keep trying to be hard, keep hanging out with the wrong people, keep doing things on the borderline between legal and illegal, keep going to the wrong places at the wrong time with the wrong people, and keep doing stuff on the Internet you are not supposed to do, and your disobedience and rebellion against God will cost you more than you have to pay, take you farther than you planned to go, and keep you longer than you planned to stay.

In the story of Samson, do not focus on Samson's hair growing back. Focus on Samson's location when his hair started growing back. Samson suffered the consequences of his wrongs in a Philistine penitentiary.

While we are suffering our consequences, however, and the enemy thinks we are broken, God is still in control. Can you imagine what Samson felt like and how he looked in that prison as a grinder? Surely, his life flashed before him. Surely, Samson thought about all that he had and all that he could have done. Surely, Samson thought about his mistakes. The enemy thought they had Samson, who was filled with regret and looked broken. However, God had the final say in Samson's case, and God has the final say in your case. God is in control!

The enemy does not have the details of God's plan for our lives. The enemy is not equal to our God. The enemy will think we are finished when God is still working His plan for our lives. "However, the hair of his head began to grow again after it was shaved off" (Judges 16:22).

When the enemy thought Samson was finished, the enemy did not see God working.

The enemy cannot see God giving you strength after you fall to the ground and look like you are out for the count. The good news in the midst of what looks like a knockout situation is that the enemy will think we are finished, but God is still working. Your hair will grow back after the enemy cuts you hair. In other words, when the enemy uses your weaknesses against you and takes action to destroy you, and you are suffering, God does not abandon you. God is still working.

How many times has the enemy sucker-punched you because you dropped your guard, but you could see and feel that God had not abandoned you and was still working in your life?

Let me tell you something else about the enemy while you are visiting with Samson in the Gaza Federal Penitentiary. The enemy will rejoice as if their idol gods are in control.

Now the lords of the Philistines assembled to offer a great sacrifice to Dagon their god, and to rejoice, for they said, 'Our god has given Samson our enemy into our hands'" (Judges 16:23).

The enemy was happy and took time to verbalize their happiness about putting Samson out of commission. The Philistines rejoiced and gave credit to their idol god Dagon. Dagon was the primary idol god for the Philistines. Why did the Philistines rejoice? Because they believed Dagon, their idol god, had stopped Samson from destroying the Philistines.

When we fall into sin and stop doing the Lord's work, the enemy rejoices. When we get discouraged and quit doing the Lord's work, the enemy rejoices. The enemy does not care about our reasons for quitting; the enemy rejoices when we quit.

Do you get it? People are constantly consulting their idol gods and looking for ways to knock God's children out of the box. People go to the palm readers, spirit guides, voodoo witches, ungodly leaders, and other demonically inspired or controlled sources, trying figure out how to stop God's children from doing God's work. The enemy will worship idols when we seem broken beyond repair.

Not only did the Philistines rejoice, but also they worshipped Dagon when Samson seemed broken beyond repair. Look at how connected the enemy is to their idol gods: "When the people saw him, they praised their god, for they said, 'Our god has given our enemy into our hands, Even the destroyer of our country, Who has slain many of us'" (Judges 16:24).

The enemy will party uncontrollably over our apparent brokenness. Keep reading. "It so happened when they were in high spirits, that they said, 'Call for Samson, that he may amuse us.' So they called for Samson from the prison, and he entertained them. And they made him stand between the pillars" (Judges 16:25).

The Philistines partied uncontrollably over Samson's apparent brokenness. They were drunk. Getting rid of Samson called for a drunken party to celebrate the fall of Samson.

Do you think your enemies are saddened when you fall into sin, lose your credibility, and are no longer doing God's work? No, they are happy that you fell on your face. They will get drunk and rejoice over your apparent brokenness.

Partying is not the end. The enemy will humiliate us when they think we are broken. Look at what the Philistines did when Samson seemed broken beyond repair: "'Call for Samson, that he may amuse us.' So they called for Samson from the prison, and he entertained them. And they made him stand between the pillars" (Judges 16:25).

They humiliated and made fun of Samson. "Bring the strong man out," they might have said, "and let us see what he can do to entertain us."

Can you picture how the enemy wants to humiliate us? "Bring the fallen preacher out; bring the fallen deacon out; bring the fallen teenager out; bring out the fallen Sunday school teacher, youth leader, children's church leader, small group leader, usher; bring out the Christian who was always talking about Jesus. We broke her, we broke him, and now he is on drugs, kicked out of college, and without his scholarship." The enemy wants to humiliate us.

"We turned him out on his eighteenth birthday. We got her crazy drunk at twenty-one, and she got into a fight, and the police arrested her. Yeah! Oh yes, did she tell you she lost her high-security clearance after that drunken episode?"

Watch your enemy. Your enemy will humiliate you when they think you are broken.

The enemy is constantly setting traps for God's children to break us down and stop us from doing God's work. Yes, sometimes we fall into those traps and we make a mistake. When we make a mistake, the enemy rejoices and tries to humiliate us when we look broken beyond repair. However, the believer's reality is all over the Bible. Here is the believer's reality:

"The hair of his head began to grow again after it was shaved off" (Judges 16:22).

Despite making a mistake, God, in His mercy, will let our hair grow back. Our hair growing back does not happen overnight; it's a slow process. In our consequences, God's mercy works.

"The LORD is compassionate and gracious, Slow to anger and abounding in lovingkindness. He will not always strive with us, Nor will He keep His anger forever. He has not dealt with us according to our sins, Nor rewarded us according to our iniquities" (Psalm 103:8–10).

"We are afflicted in every way, but not crushed; perplexed, but not despairing; persecuted, but not forsaken; struck down, but not destroyed" (2 Corinthians 4:8–9).

"For I am confident of this very thing, that He who began a good work in you will perfect it until the day of Christ Jesus" (Philippians 1:6).

The believer's reality is that even when we make a mistake and fall into the enemy's trap, God is merciful, and God will never leave us or forsake us. God works circumstances to get our attention, to get us to repent, to get us restored, and to get us back into service. God is with us. "Just as a father has compassion on his children, So the LORD has compassion on those who fear Him. For He Himself knows our frame; He is mindful that we are but dust" (Psalm 103:13–14).

Despite his humiliation by the Philistines and despite looking like he was beaten, Samson knew he could count on God for another chance. Despite Samson's spiritual weaknesses and the numerous distractions from his calling, Samson saw God's mercy window open.

"Then Samson said to the boy who was holding his hand, 'Let me feel the pillars on which the house rests, that I may lean against them.' Now the house was full of men and women, and all the lords of the Philistines were there. And about 3,000 men and women were on the roof looking on while Samson was amusing them" (Judges 16:26–27).

You cannot see God's mercy window of opportunity if your spirit is broken. If you keep beating yourself up—if you ask God to forgive you but you continue to kick yourself—you cannot see God's mercy. If you constantly fill your head with negative self-talk, you will not see God's mercy.

Here are some examples of negative self-talk:

- I cannot do anything right.
- I cannot live up to their standards.
- I will never be perfect.
- Even if I study, I will never get good grades.
- I just cannot keep a job.
- Nobody understands me.
- I just do not fit in with good people.
- I just cannot forgive this time, so why try.
- I am a failure.

Because Samson, in his rock-bottom condition, looked up to God, he saw God's mercy window. No matter how many mistakes you have made, no matter how bad you think your situation is, and no matter how discouraged, disappointed, and disturbed you are, if you look up to God, He will show you His mercy window.

What did Samson do when he saw God's mercy window open? He prayed in faith.

"Then Samson called to the LORD and said, 'O Lord GOD, please remember me and please strengthen me just this time, O God, that I may at once be avenged of the Philistines for my two eyes'" (Judges 16:28).

Samson's including that revenge thing in his prayer may bother you; I know it bothered me. Samson's revenge agenda limited his effectiveness. All of Samson's fights in the book of Judges were because of something that someone did to him in connection to the enemy's women.

Samson's human dust slipping into his last prayer to God may bother you, but remember this: "Just as a father has compassion on his children, So the LORD has compassion on those who fear Him. For He Himself knows our frame; He is mindful that we are but dust" (Psalm 103:13–14).

Some human dust got onto some of your prayers, and God still worked with you. You were tore up from the floor up. You were trying to reconcile the difference between what you were thinking and feeling on the inside and what you were doing on the outside. You were a ball of confusion, and you decided to pray. Human dust was all over your prayer, and you did not know how to pray as you should, but the Spirit of the Living God took your old dusty prayer and interceded for you with groanings too deep for words. God, who searches the hearts and knows the mind of the Holy Spirit, received your old dusty prayer, as the Holy Spirit presented it before God (Romans 8:26–27).

Oh yes, you had some human dust on your prayers, and God looked at your heart and saw what you really meant, and He heard and answered your prayers.

This obviously was the case with Samson. Samson prayed in faith, with some human dust in his prayer. After Samson prayed, what did he do? Did Samson doubt God? No, Samson acted in faith. "Samson grasped the two middle pillars on which the house rested, and braced himself against them, the one with his right hand and the other with his left" (Judges 16:29).

Samson saw God's mercy window open and prayed in faith. Samson got busy with an act of faith. He knew that God was with him, and Samson got himself in position and anticipated God's power working in and through him one last time.

Hurry and look at what happened next! "And Samson said, 'Let me die with the Philistines!' And he bent with all his might so that the house fell on the lords and all the people who were in it. So the dead whom he killed at his death were more than those whom he killed in his life" (Judges 16:30).

What do you see here? In his death, God's mercy window gave Samson fulfillment.

"Let me die with the Philistines!" Samson died fulfilling his calling. He died fighting the people God called him to fight. This time, Samson knew he would not come out of the battle. Samson closed his eyes, fulfilling his calling. *Let me die doing what God called me to do in the first place.*

In Samson's death, God continued to break the Philistine hold on Israel. Look at who died in Samson's final battle.

Judges 16:27 said that the lords of the Philistines were in the house. (The five lords of the Philistines were the ones who paid Delilah to get Samson's secret.)

Judges 16:27 also said that around three thousand men and women were on the roof of the house, looking on as the Philistines humiliated Samson. Three thousand were on the roof of the temple to Dagon, or in the upper seating area, and other people were near were Samson was. We don't know the total number who died that day, but we know over three thousand people died in Samson's last battle.

What can you count on God for? Answer this question before you finish this final chapter.

What do you know about God's window of mercy? (Psalm 100:5; Ephesians 2:1–5; Lamentations 3:22–23).

Stop beating yourself up and trying to use self-punishment to relieve your guilt and shame. Only Jesus can relieve your guilt and shame. When you go to God with a godly sorrow, when you connect your emotions to your confession of sin, and you are truly sorry and turn away from your sins, God will have mercy on you.

"He who conceals his transgressions will not prosper, But he who confesses and forsakes them will find compassion" (Proverbs 28:13).

Which of God's windows of opportunity is open before you today?

If you missed God's main window, do you see God's mercy window?

If you still have God's main window before you, what are you doing to seize the opportunity?

Pray so that you do not miss any more of God's windows of ministry opportunity.

Here is a personal prayer to help:

Dear Lord, thank you for being the God of all mercy and giving me another chance. I admit I had some days, just like Samson, where I was distracted and operated independently of you, but now I see the mercy window of ministry opportunity that you opened just for me. Lord, I do not want to repeat my past mistakes and blow off your work as insignificant. Therefore, keep me close to you in prayer, keep me in fellowship with the right people, and keep me in Your Word. Father, as I humbly serve You, I desire total satisfaction in you and for you to find satisfaction in me. I love you. In the name of Jesus, I pray. Amen.

Printed in the United States
By Bookmasters